◆ FriesenPress

One Printers Way
Altona, MB R0G 0B0
Canada

www.friesenpress.com

Copyright © 2024 by Frank Banfield
First Edition — 2024

All rights reserved.

No part of this publication may be reproduced in any form, or by any means, electronic or mechanical, including photocopying, recording, or any information browsing, storage, or retrieval system, without permission in writing from FriesenPress.

ISBN
978-1-03-917264-7 (Hardcover)
978-1-03-917263-0 (Paperback)
978-1-03-917265-4 (eBook)

BIOGRAPHY & AUTOBIOGRAPHY, PERSONAL MEMOIRS

Distributed to the trade by The Ingram Book Company

To Freddy (Gabby)
Mischief isn't the same without you.

To Abi
 Is the food better up there?

TABLE OF CONTENTS

Introduction vii

Vunga's Early Years 1

1	MALARIA BLUES	3
2	SUGAR MILL SHENANIGANS	9
3	THE GREAT STAIR RACE	15
4	VUNGA LEARNS YOU DON'T MESS WITH MOTHERS	19
5	SAVING GRANDMA'S NUTMEG HARVEST	23
6	AUNT MARLENE'S PERFECT FIASCO	29
7	BELMONT MISCHIEF	39
8	POLLY THE SQUEALER	45
9	THE CURE	53
10	HUNTING THE GUNDY CRAB	59

Vunga's Teenish Years 67

11	VUNGA'S VERY TALL TAXMAN TALE	69
12	THE GREAT FISHMAN	75
13	ZORRO WANNABES MEET THE SHANGO WOMAN	83

Vunga Leaves his Beloved Island . . . 91

14	GRENADA FAREWELL	93

INTRODUCTION
A HEALING COLLABORATION

You might wonder: what do an eighty-seven-year-old writer
and an eighteen-year-old artist have in common?

When Frank finished writing the tales featuring himself and his late brother as two incorrigible mischief-makers, his London Writers Society critique group enthusiastically encouraged him to find an illustrator. And so, the search was on. A pensioner of humble means, Frank suggested the book be a kind of collaboration. Frank would pay the publication costs and a modest fee for each of the drawings and author and illustrator would share credit and royalties equally.

About two years into the search, and after many rejections, Frank invited Abi, one of his students, to illustrate the tales. She replied that her sister was the artist in the family. And that is how Eva Parada came to illustrate Vunga and Gabby's sometimes real and sometimes imaginary island adventures. The project became a tribute to both the author's and the illustrator's lost siblings.

THE AUTHOR

Vunga: Tales of an Island Boy is a fictional memoir based on the quasi-true adventures of Frank Banfield (a.k.a. Vunga) and his younger brother Freddy (a.k.a. Gabby). But don't look for Freddy in the real world. Freddy died at the age of seven as the result of a bullying incident at school.

It happened during recess. The boys were playing marbles with two other students. A dispute arose when one of the boys tried to steal Frank's coveted white, speckled marble.

Freddy, who always looked out for his sickly older brother, tried to take it back. The bully punched Freddy so hard his appendix ruptured. Because Freddy suffered from chronic appendicitis, he died a few days later.

The loss of his younger brother deeply affected Frank. His parents sent him to live with one of his favourite older sisters. Unable to have children of their own, Ermintrude and her husband, Wilfred, welcomed the grief-stricken boy into their home. Suffering from chronic malaria, he spent the mosquito season with yet another sister, who was a nurse. During his long convalescence he imagined the many adventures awaiting him beyond the sick room. As he grew older, and became ever more of a handful, Frank's family passed him around until he finally went back to the family farm at the age of twelve. When Frank turned seventeen, his aging parents, who could no longer cope with their increasingly mischievous son, shipped him off to Canada to live with an older brother who had just graduated from the University of Sudbury.

Years later, still pining for Freddy and still dreaming up all kinds of adventures he and his brother might have enjoyed, Frank began writing his Vunga tales. Enter Gabby, the wise young boy with an old soul.

THE ILLUSTRATOR

Eva Leilany Parada was fifteen years old when Frank approached her about drawing the cover for the Vunga tales. At that time, Eva had just lost her older sister to cancer and was going through her own grieving process. She knew that the stories in Vunga were about the childhood adventures of Frank and his younger brother Freddy, who had passed away as well.

After Eva presented her ideas for the cover, Frank asked her to draw the illustrations for the book. This experience has not only allowed Eva to grow as an artist, but has also allowed her to pay tribute to her older sister. Illustrating Vunga and Gabby's unforgettable adventures served as a reminder of the many good times she enjoyed with her sister.

The loss of a sibling is hard to overcome, especially when that loss happens at such an early age. However, the heartwarming memories of time spent together—even if it meant getting in trouble—fill a broken heart with laughter, love, and the hope that one day you will be reunited again! This is what Vunga represents to Eva.

VUNGA'S EARLY YEARS

1

MALARIA BLUES

In the tropics there are two seasons: the dry season and the rainy season. But for people like me, there is a third season. Somewhere between the dry season and the rainy season, there is the mosquito season, or, as I know it, the malaria season. In a way, I am named after it. On the island, practically every boy has a nickname. Mine is Vunga, which is a kind of mosquito that causes malaria. It is also a kind of mosquito that buzzes around, annoying people.

In Grenada, everyone knows when to hang the nets from the ceiling of every bedroom. They envelop each bed and protect us while we sleep. For most people, the bringing out of the nets is enough to make them feel safe from these nasty creatures. But for me, this annual event strikes dread into my little heart.

In between illnesses, I live on the farm. There, my younger brother Gabby and I are inseparable. People who don't know us think we're twins, only I'm skinny and he has muscles everywhere. For us it is a time of wonderment as we are constantly making discoveries in this place of lustrous green pastures, sugarcane fields, and coconut trees. Vast amounts of fruit trees of every kind grow on the farm. It is the ideal place for any boy, especially a mischievous one like me, to grow up.

Even though we know malaria season is coming soon, we don't know the exact moment it will start. It is the furthest thing from my mind as Gabby and I practise our writing skills in Mother's shop. I watch as he struggles to copy each letter just right. He's only six, but he can write tons better than I can. My slate is covered with huge, uneven, misshapen letters. Mother clucks her tongue.

"Vunga, I don't think you're concentrating on what you're doing," she admonishes.

In fact, I'm daydreaming about sliding down the slope behind the house on coconut tree fronds, and I've begun to feel sweaty.

"Mom, I feel hot."

"Are you sure?" she asks and comes over and places her hand on my forehead. She shakes her head. "You have a fever," she says, then calls out, "La-La, bring the bitter cup and get things ready for Vunga and you to go to the Belmont house."

La-La lives in a small cabin on top of the hill across from our farmhouse. Every day she walks the four miles to Belmont to take care of me. La-La is a heavy, round-faced woman with a big mole in the middle of her left cheek. Whenever I grab it, she laughs and says, "That is my signal that you're well again and I can look after the other little ones." I have four younger siblings back at the farm. She also sings hymns and when she can't remember the words, the syllables "La, la, la" replace them. And thus, she came to be known as La-La.

La-La appears with the wooden cup carved out of the wood of an excelsa tree and holds it to my lips. "Come baby, drink it up," she says then puts her hand on my cheek. "My, my, you really hot."

She picks me up and carries me to my room and covers me with a sheet.

"La-La, why the net don't keep me safe?" I ask.

"Sweet child, some of them mosquitoes, they so thin they can come right through the net."

"But they only bite me," I complain. "They don't care about Pounda and Slingshot."

"Those older brothers of yours, they too tough," she says, "not nice and tender like you."

"I want to be tough, too."

"Hush, child, get some sleep now."

An hour later, Dad hitches a donkey to the cart and drives me and La-La to the house in Belmont, where Aunt Allie, my sister who's a nurse, lives with two of our other grown-up sisters, Marlene and Clara. I call them *aunt* or *auntie* because they are adults.

La-La carries me into the house and lays me on the wicker loveseat in the living room. In a few minutes, she returns with a wet cloth and puts it on my head while she makes up a bed for me.

"All right, baby," she says and picks me up and carries me to the room with a window that looks out onto the road.

La-La brings a chair up next to my bed and begins to sing to me. When Aunt Allie walks into my room, she puts a thermometer in my mouth.

"Child, you have one bad fever," she says. "La-La, make him a thin chicken broth and feed it to him slowly."

As soon as La-La goes to the kitchen, Aunt Allie sits on the side of the bed and cradles my head in her arm.

"Don't you worry, Vunga. I'll get you through this."

"Auntie, I feel cold."

She leaves the room for a few minutes and returns with a big cover and wraps me up in it. La-La brings the soup and feeds me with a spoon. I lie in her arms shaking. She hugs me tight. I close my eyes and the room disappears.

One day, I feel something cold on my face as I stir into consciousness. The bedsheet under me is soaking wet. I vaguely remember shivering and being very hot. Hot as if on fire.

I groan and stir. A voice, as if from a distance, says, "Shush, shush, baby," then begins to sing. "Rock-a-bye baby on a treetop . . ."

A tear trickles down my cheek as I become aware of her presence. My La-La is here with me. I look up and see the big mole on her beautiful round face and think: *She is always there when I need her.* I smile weakly at her and she smiles back. She bends forward and kisses my brow.

"Yes, sweet child, me here with you as always," she says. Then, reaching down to check the sheet, she exclaims, "It soak right to the mattress. We need to change you and the bedclothes."

"I don't feel good, La-La. Was it bad?"

La-La knows I mean the sickness and replies, "Baby, me been here with you through all your hot and cold times, praying to the good Lord to help you through it." Then, looking up, she says, "Thank you, Lord, for getting me baby through it once again."

As she soothes my brow with her hand, she consoles me in country talk.

"Me know you weak. Me go and get the cot to put you on while me get nice clean sheets and turn the mattress so you have a dry bed to rest in." She pokes my tummy. "That all right with you?"

I look up and smile. "I doing okay, La-La."

She hurries off to get the cot, which she brings back and puts near the bed. Then she lifts me up and places me on it.

"You comfortable?" A worried look comes to her face. "You haven't eat much for a long time now. You like some water?"

"A little." I smile up at her. "Thanks, La-La."

La-La gives me that broad-faced grin of hers that lights up the room. Then she disappears down the hall. She returns with the water and holds my head up so I can drink. She places the cup to my lips so I can sip the bitter water to fight the fever.

"Slowly, baby. That's enough. Now lie back down while me take the wet things to the laundry house. When me get back, me read to you."

"I like that."

"Maybe you try eating some paw-paw, cause me don't think you stomach goin' to take anything else."

"If you feel it good for me."

"Baby, it's good for you and it goin' help you get strong again."

She walks out of the room singing, "La, la, la . . ." and I know everything is going to be all right.

2

SUGAR MILL SHENANIGANS

After breakfast, the three older ones—Lolli, Pounda, and Slingshot—change out of their work clothes, grab their schoolbooks, and head for town. Mother opens her shop, a kind of mini general store selling everything from candy to cheese to fabric. Gabby and I sit at a table behind the sales counter and practise writing on our slates. I pick up the chalk with my left hand and begin copying letters. Between customers I get a whack on my knuckles. No wonder I hate writing.

"Child, you know better. Use your other hand. If not, you'll never be able to go to school."

I look up at my mother. "Mom, it's too hard for me. My hand hurts."

"Son, I know. But that's how the rules are. I used to teach before I married your father. The schools will not accept you. Please try the hardest you can. Your right hand will get used to it. Will you try?"

"Yes, Mom."

After a while Mother says, "Boys, you can go play now until lunch. Vunga, no mischief!" She wags her pointing finger at me. Gabby smiles knowingly.

She hands us each a mint jawbreaker from the big jar on the counter. We bound out of the shop, past the rabbit hutch and chicken coop, running our right hands along the doors and calling out "Hiya!" to stir up the animals into a kind of sniffing and clucking frenzy. Then we head to the backyard to decide what to do. From where we are standing, I can see the roof of Dad's sugar mill. I think: *What fun we could have pretending to make sugar.* I tap Gabby on the shoulder.

"Let's explore the sugar mill," I suggest.

"What for? Dad said it doesn't start up for two weeks."

"So now's the best time," I reason. "No one's around."

We run down the path between the outhouse and the pigpen, then turn right, passing the cattle stalls. When we reach the mill, we discover the padlock on the door is open. That means Dad has started to get the mill ready. We walk inside and stand before a wheel about four times my height. A wide belt connects this giant wheel to a much smaller wheel that grinds the cane and squeezes the juice out of it. A thought pops into my head. *Wouldn't it be fun to slide down the belt from the big wheel to the little one?*

As I look around trying to figure out how to get to the top of the big wheel, Gabby calls out, "Hey, look at this!"

He's pointing to three large, black, cast-iron cauldrons across from the big wheel.

"Wow, they're gigantic!" I explode and run over to them.

Gabby drags a wooden crate to where I'm standing. He hops onto the box and examines the huge vats. "You think we can slide down into one of those?" he asks.

I shake my head. The vats are deep. "Nah," I tell him. "How will we get out?"

I look up and see three very long ladles suspended on big hooks above the cauldrons. Gabby follows my gaze.

"You think we can reach those big spoons?" he asks.

"I don't know, they seem awfully high to me."

"Maybe we can climb to the top of the big wheel," he says hopefully.

I know my brother. It's not about the spoons. "You really want to slide down that belt, don't you?" I ask him.

"Why not? It'll be lots of fun."

For once, I am the cautious one.

"What if we fall," I ask him, "then what?"

Then typically, when blocked, Gabby switches gears. "Let's look for something to knock one of the big spoons down." His face lights up. "Then we can pretend we're making sugar." He points to some steps at the base of the smaller wheel that lead to the belt. "We can get up these easy and walk to the bigger wheel on the broad belt," he says. "From there maybe we can get the spoons down."

We scamper up the steps. I climb up to the belt and call for Gabby to join me.

"This is fun," I say in a voice filled with promise, but my bravado soon gives way to misgivings.

With two of us jogging along it, the belt begins to sway, first slightly, then shakier and shakier. Scared, I drop to my knees. I call out:

"Gabby, you all right?"

"I think it going to break." His voice is trembling. "I going to crawl back and get off."

"You stay there and I'll come to where you are and help you down."

No sooner are we both safely on the ground than we discover a long pole with a hook on the end leaning against the engine that drives the belt.

"Look," I say, grabbing it, "we can use this to get the big spoons down."

On the third try, the long-handled spoon nearest us clanks down to the floor of the mill. I pick it up and step onto the platform above the cauldron to stir the imaginary sugar. Gabby is instantly by my side.

"Can I try?" he pleads.

I surrender the spoon and climb up onto the edge of the next cauldron. I imagine I'm in the circus. *The one, the only, the amazing Vunga walks the edge of a giant vat filled to the brim with boiling oil.* I walk faster and faster until I'm actually running.

"Look, try this!" I yell to Gabby.

I run even faster, trying to impress him. Suddenly, I lose my balance and tumble to the bottom of the cauldron, hitting my head hard on the metal surface. I let out a howl and begin bawling at the top of my lungs. Gabby stretches the ladle down to me but I'm too busy with my misery to have the presence of mind to grab it. Suddenly, I hear a booming voice.

"What in the world are you two doing?"

Gabby is crying as he answers Dad's question. He's still clutching the giant spoon. "I want to help Vunga," he explains. "I want to stop his head from bleeding. Daddy, help me save him."

Dad leans over the edge of the cauldron, reaches down, grabs my hands, and pulls me to safety. "You should know better," he scolds. "You could get badly hurt fooling around with the mill. Whatever possessed you to bring your little brother here in the first place?"

"I know, Dad," I say, sniffling, my head hanging down.

He looks at the cut on the back of my head and presses a handkerchief to the wound. "Thank you, Lord," he says, his voice trembling ever so slightly, "for sparing my son yet again."

"Gabby tell me to take the ladle down so we can play making sugar with it," I say, trying to shift some of the blame onto my little brother.

Dad scowls. "Yes," he says, "but you're always the one who comes up with the crazy ideas. Your mother will decide what punishment is best for the two of you. Now get back to the house."

As we head back up to the house, we try very hard to suppress the smiles rising on our faces. Mom is always soft on punishment.

3

THE GREAT STAIR RACE

It is still dark. I hear the pattering of feet as the house comes alive. This is no surprise to me; I hear it every morning. When I try to follow the others to be part of the commotion, Mother whispers to me, "Sweetie, they're going to milk the cattle. The milkmaid will be here soon to take the milk to town."

I whisper back, "Why, Mom?"

"Because they sell the milk to people who live where there are no cows."

"But, Mom . . ."

She cuts me off. "You're too small."

I'm not small. I'm seven! I hear clanging coming from the outdoor kitchen and ask, "What they doing?"

She puts a finger on her lips and utters, "Shush, the baby is sleeping and I have to help them." She ruffles my hair. "Now, go back to bed and not another word out of you."

I pout. "Not fair!"

I stomp back to my bed, where I sleep with two of my older brothers, the same ones who are now on their way to milk the cattle. Having the bed to myself, I lie across it and continue fretting, even though there's no one to hear.

"Why they always get to do the fun things? Mom makes me learn writing and all that hard stuff. I hate writing."

I continue feeling sorry for myself until I hear the cock crow. All of a sudden, I feel very tired and roll onto my side. I'm just dozing off when Gabby comes running into the room and jumps up on the bed.

"Why you still lying down? You sick?" he asks, his face beaming as he bounces up and down, shaking the whole bed.

I rub my eyes and reply, "No. Just thinking." I hop out of bed and grab his hand. "Let's go to the kitchen for breakfast."

"Last one down the stairs is a cow," Gabby shouts, yanking his hand free.

I quickly dash past Gabby. With my brother in hot pursuit, I grab the railing and head down the stairs, which lead outside to the kitchen. A small cement patio separates the kitchen from the main house. I miss a step and go tumbling to the bottom just as Mother steps out of the kitchen. My puny body slams into her legs, saving my head from hitting the concrete floor. While I cry and wobble, holding onto my shins, Gabby calmly walks past me into the kitchen. Once inside the doorway, he turns and calls back, "You the cow!" He bends forward laughing.

"Cow, cow, cow!" I yell back.

"No way!" Gabby shouts. "You still all outside. My whole body inside."

The taunt hurts. My heart pounds as I try to figure out a way to get even. Mother pulls me up onto my feet, shaking her head.

"Son, you'll be the death of me yet. Is anything hurting?"

"My arms and my shins." I feel about my head. "Only one bump here."

I touch the bump with a finger as I stare at Gabby's grinning face. Mother pulls up my shirtsleeves to check for bruises.

"Nothing serious," she declares. "Now go sit down for breakfast before the others get back with the milk."

Gabby comes and sits next to me. I decide to ignore him.

He looks at my bruised knee and asks, "Does it hurt?" I remain silent. He puts his arm around my shoulder. "You really got down quick," he teases, "just like a mosquito diving through the net." Then he asks, "A tie?"

My face bursts into a big grin. "A tie!" I agree.

And just like that, we are best of friends again.

4

VUNGA LEARNS YOU DON'T MESS WITH MOTHERS

One day I decide we should go into the pigpen and play with the baby pigs. They are about a week old and just begging for our attention. As we come around the outdoor kitchen to get to the pigs, Gabby asks, "What if the mother pig don't want us playing with her children?"

"Why not? We're children too."

"Oh." He doesn't sound convinced.

"She'll be happy to have us play with her children," I assure him.

I open the gate and he follows me into the pigpen. The mother pig is lying down. As we approach, she grunts and struggles to her feet.

She charges.

Seeing the danger, I push Gabby and shout, "Run, Gabby, run!"

Just then the sow butts me in my rear, sending me headfirst into the mud. Panic sets in as I try to get up and slip again while the pig is squealing at the top of her lungs. She makes another lunge at me as I scamper on all fours to get away. She is one angry mother.

"Faster, Vunga," Gabby yells.

Hearing all the racket, Mother appears at the edge of the pigsty in time to see the mother pig push me right out of the pigpen. I land on my back while Gabby comes to my rescue with a piece of wood. He swings it at her head, just missing her. The sow backs up and checks each of her litter before lying down again.

Mother comes down to where we are, grabs the backs of our shirts, and maneuvers us up the slope to the cistern. There she strips off our clothes, then opens the tap to wash the stinky goo off our bodies. Afterward, she stands us in the sun to dry while she fetches some clean clothes from the house.

"You know now that mothers do not like others near their babies," Gabby declares with an air of authority.

"How you know that?"

"This happen when I try to play with a little chick once," he says, pointing at a scar on his hand.

"Why you didn't tell me?"

"I just tell you now."

Mother returns with our clothes and a caution. "No more bothering the pigs and the other animals on the farm. You can get hurt if you get a sow angry. Well, a cow is much bigger and has horns. They can cut you badly. Come into the shop and practise your writing."

Gabby and I sigh heavily. Maybe if we're lucky, a customer will show up and we'll be able to sneak outside.

5

SAVING GRANDMA'S NUTMEG HARVEST

One day, Gabby and I are practising our writing when Ma'am Casteau comes into the shop. She is on her way back from the post office in town. She gives Mother a letter.

Mother thanks Ma'am Casteau and gives her a jawbreaker for her trouble. As soon as she leaves, Mother tears open the envelope. The arrival of a personal letter is an exciting event and we expect her to share the news, but when she finishes reading, Mother takes our slates from us and puts them away.

"Children, go to the potato beds below the back pasture and bring your father. Tell him it's important."

Gabby and I run down the hill, through the coconut trees to the bottomland.

"Dad, Mother got a letter and wants you to come right away," I tell him.

"Mom looks worried," Gabby adds.

We hurry back to the house. Knowing Dad has trouble with reading and writing, Mother reads the letter out loud. Gabby and I are all ears.

My dearest daughter,
I do not want to be a burden to you, but your father is very ill and I, too, am in poor health. As you know, it is nutmeg harvesting time. I do not want to impose, but I am desperate. Could you come and bring a little help to pick up the nutmeg so the mace will not rot on the ground?

Your ever-loving Mother

It takes only a few minutes for my parents to decide that Pounda and Slingshot are old enough to take care of the farm. La-La will cook meals and make sure the boys get to school on time. Lolli and Jasmine will stay at the Belmont house with Marlene and Allie and Clara. That means Gabby and Double-R—he's four—and I will help out at the nutmeg plantation along with our parents. La-La makes cheese sandwiches and *pun-pun* for us to take on our trip. We love the sweet-potato pie and our excitement rises as the time approaches for the bus to arrive. We gather in the front yard to wait for it.

Double-R starts to fuss. Gabby picks up a leaf and pretends it's a bird. Double-R picks one up too and follows him around the yard, chirping. Mother smiles at how easily Gabby engages our little brother in play.

"That child was born wise," she says.

"What about me?" I pout.

"You, Vunga? Hah! You were born mischief." She laughs and I laugh too. Then she ruffles my hair to show she loves me no matter how I was born.

Within a few minutes, the bus pulls up in front of our house. As usual, it's pretty full. The bus has no sides and no doors. Dad makes sure we little ones are not on any end seats where we can fall out. As the youngest, Double-R sits on Mother's lap, while Gabby and I sit with Dad. Gabby and I soon fall asleep from boredom. Dad wakes us when the bus stops at a little store. Some people get off so we are able to sit with Mother and Double-R. We devour La-La's sandwiches as the bus continues toward Grenville. Upon arrival, Dad goes into the depot and makes a call.

"Your Uncle Basil will pick us up in about twenty minutes," he says when he returns. "Let's sit under that tree until he gets here."

Gabby and I are too tired of sitting and decide to run around the tree while the others enjoy the cool breeze and shade. Of course, Double-R wants to run with us.

The drive to Uncle Basil's home does not take as long as I expected. Maybe that's because we three boys fell asleep within a minute of getting into the car. When we finally arrive, it's dark. Mother hurries us into the house to meet the rest of the family, but all I want is to dig into the curry dish that I smelled when we walked in. Mother must read my mind because she goes into the kitchen to help Aunt Mildred dish out our supper.

After the meal, Uncle Basil introduces us to his sons: Toe-Toe, the older of the two boys, and his younger brother, Me-Too. We play for a while, then Mother brings us to another room to sleep. Dad peeks his head in the door to say goodnight.

"Don't make any noise when you wake up. Your uncle and auntie like to sleep in a little on Saturday morning."

I hear a cock "*Cok-kioko!*" and right away I'm up trying to figure out where I am. I look out the window. It's still dark, but I can see that the ground is flat, not like Calivigny, which is full of hills and valleys. Then I remember where we are. I also remember what Dad said about not making noise, so I quietly pull on my clothes.

Gabby stirs then raises his head. "That you?"

"Shush," I whisper, putting a finger to my lips.

"What you doin'?" he whispers.

"I want to see outside," I whisper back as I quietly climb out the window and ease myself down to the ground.

I look back and Gabby is climbing out too. He joins me, walking around the house. I run toward a little shed. As we approach it, I hear cackling and realize there are fowls living in the hut just like at home. A dog starts barking. Gabby grabs my hand just as a light comes on in the house.

"Who there?" a voice calls out urgently. Then even more urgently, "Who there? I have a gun. Show yourself now or I shoot."

"Don't shoot, Uncle Basil. It's me, Vunga. And Gabby," I plead as we walk up to the house. By the time we get inside, everyone is up.

Dad grabs my right ear while admonishing me. "What did I tell you last night?"

"Not to make noise. Aw, that hurts, Dad. Ow, ow!"

"Daddy, I'm here, too," Gabby says. As usual, he's trying to save my butt by claiming to be part of the mischief. And as usual, it works. Dad lets go of my ear, turns to Mother, and asks, "What are we going to do with this boy?"

Mother comes over and hugs me. She replies, "He'll grow out of it soon, dear. He just needs a little more time."

I'm grateful for her support, though looking back, I'm glad she didn't know then that I never would—grow out of being a troublemaker, that is.

"Look at what a bad example he is to his younger brother." Dad shakes his head.

"I do it, too, Daddy," Gabby insists, jumping up and down.

Just then, Aunt Mildred calls us in to breakfast and it's as if our early-morning mischief never happened. After filling our hungry stomachs, Uncle Basil drives us to our grandparents' house. Grandma comes out to greet us and tells us Grandpa is at the hospital and won't be home for a while. When Grandma comes to hug me, she holds me at arm's length.

"Goodness, you have a lot of bruises, child," she says.

I shrug my shoulders.

"He's a very active child," Dad tells her. "We'll try to keep him busy."

"That's good," Grandma says. "We have a lot to do here. I'm sure we'll *all* be very busy." Somehow, she manages to give all us children *the look* at the same time.

She quickly makes assignments. Dad and Uncle Basil will use poles to shake the branches of the trees and Toe-Toe, Me-Too, Gabby, and I will gather pods and put them into two big baskets. Mother and Aunt Mildred will separate the pods and the mace from the nutmeg. Double-R will stay with Mother and put the pods in the bin for the pigs.

It's wild watching the nutmeg pods rain down as the two men shake the branches violently with their poles. The sweat runs down their faces and soaks their clothes, making them stick to their skin.

Meanwhile, Gabby and I begin picking up the pods and throwing them into our basket. After a while, I bend over with my legs apart so I can throw the pods between my legs, into the basket behind me. Before long we forget about the basket and start flinging the pods at each other, weaving, and dodging the projectiles. Our laughter is shattered by Dad's booming voice.

"What in the world is going on? Look at your cousins, how they do it."

All is quiet as we look to where Toe-Toe and Me-Too are working. They're scooping the pods in both hands and dropping them into the basket. Their basket is almost full while ours is not even halfway to the top.

"I guess we got carried away," I say as I turn to my brother with a guilty face.

Gabby grins endearingly and all is forgiven. We begin to do like our cousins and easily fill one basket and then begin another. By lunchtime we have filled many baskets. We all sit on the lawn to eat beef stew with hunks of lard bread. Afterward some neighbours come by and everyone pitches in to help with the harvest. When all the work is done, we fill up on Grandma's roti and curried chicken, which we top off with nutmeg bark preserves.

After church on Sunday, all of us children play hide-and-seek and other games while the grownups finish picking the pods. On Monday we all help separate the outer pods from the nutmeg and then the mace from the nutmeg seed. By this time, all the mischief is gone out of me. I'm very tired and can hardly wait to eat supper and drop into bed. Dad walks by me as I sit waiting for my food. He ruffles my hair, looks down at me, and says:

"I'm very proud of you, son. You and your brother have done more than was expected of you."

Praise from Dad is rare. Mother says even though we fell asleep on the bus ride back from Grenville, we both smiled all the way home.

6

AUNT MARLENE'S PERFECT FIASCO

I'll never forget Aunt Marlene's "big day." In order to understand how it became Aunt Marlene's "biggest fiasco ever," there's something you have to understand about one of my favourite adult sisters. Auntie is a Perfectionist with a capital *P*—or maybe make that PERFECTIONIST, full caps. Whenever I think about that day, I break out in a sweat. It's as if it's unfolding right before my eyes.

Aunt Marlene is home in Calivigny on one of her visits from the Belmont house. She's all excited about a man she met in town a while back.

"Bertrand and I will be getting married right after the mosquito season," she announces. "No one wants to be bitten by mosquitoes or shaking with ague on their wedding night."

"Good point," Dad says, then asks, "When's the big day?" He chuckles. It's easy for him to stay calm. There are lots of "big days" around here. After all, there are five older girls in the family, plus Lolli and Jasmine, who are close in age to me.

"The week after malaria season ends, of course," Aunt Marlene replies, giving me a wink. "I've made arrangements to tie the knot at the Scot Kirk in St. George's. The church is right across the street from the hotel where we'll be spending our honeymoon."

Dad nods his approval. As assistant manager of the hotel, she will surely receive a huge discount. He smiles proudly then heads toward the shop to tell Mother it's time to make another wedding dress.

My sister is a born organizer. Aunt Marlene itemizes every detail and makes drawings of the pulpit and where we'll all be standing or sitting the day of the big event. She also makes copies for everyone in the procession and sits down with each person in the wedding party, including Gabby and me. Gabby is to be the ring bearer and I'm in charge of holding the veil as she walks to and from the altar. She constantly emphasizes that everything must be *perfect*.

Although Gabby is only six, he and Aunt Marlene seem to be chatting like two adults. As Aunt Marlene explains how to carry the ring without dropping it Gabby offers suggestions of his own, like holding the box tightly in his fist or putting it in his pants pocket. After her chat with Gabby, Aunt Marlene calls me over. There's a slight frown on her face. She bends forward and cautions, "Vunga, you have to be at your best. No mischief. Do you understand?"

I nod my head and shrug my shoulders noncommittally. "Why not?" I ask.

Of course, I know why not. But I can't help teasing her when she's being so serious.

She puts her hands on her hips. "Because I want everything to be absolutely *perfect!*" She sighs and ruffles my hair. It's her way of saying, *"I know you're teasing me, but you'd better get it right, or else."*

I smile up at her with mischief swirling in my eyes. Aunt Marlene must be a bit of a mind-reader.

"Vunga, don't you dare!" she admonishes. "Promise?"

"Promise," I parrot back, striving to appear the picture of innocence. And I am innocent — of any *intentional* wrongdoing. But I know myself. Things just happen when I'm involved. I can't explain it any other way.

Aunt Marlene continues.

"Your job is to hold the veil up and keep it from dragging on the floor and getting all dirty."

My seven-year-old heart sinks as I try to figure out how I'm supposed to keep it from dragging on the floor. I know it once belonged to Grandma Marshall. If any harm comes to it, I'm doomed.

"Yes, ma'am," I say, sincerely serious.

Aunt Marlene smiles and goes off in search of Lolli and Jasmine. Does she really think I will be able to perform my duties to perfection?

As usual, Gabby and I take every chance to play since we both know I'll soon be overcome with malaria. That means I'll be sent to the Belmont house until just before the wedding. Aunt Marlene knows this too. Every Sunday afternoon, she comes to Calivigny and makes us practise our walk up the aisle using a tablecloth as a prop. She gives me very detailed instructions.

"Make sure you hold these two corners of the veil *just so.*"

Gabby stands stock-still with the tablecloth on his head as Auntie demonstrates the holding position.

"Now you try it," she says, handing me the two corners.

She hums "Here Comes the Bride" as Gabby slowly walks forward. I'm thinking: *Why am I doing this when what I really want to do is eat some of those freshly picked plums on the table?* I bump into a chair and tumble onto the floor.

"Vunga," Aunt Marlene chides, frowning with her hands on her hips, "the sooner you learn how to walk behind me, the sooner you won't need to practise. It must be *perfect*."

"I know, Auntie."

What I really want to say is, "*I want to go play with Gabby. I can't help thinking these thoughts and bumping into things.*"

The malaria season comes and goes. After a thorough examination, Nurse Allie declares me healthy—except for the usual bruises and bumps, of course. This makes Aunt Marlene happy as she's anxious to resume her wedding day rehearsals.

On the morning of the wedding, we are all up when we hear the cock crow. It will be a long day. The ceremony will take place at four o'clock in the afternoon. I lie in my bed listening to the commotion my three sisters are making. It's nice, as they're usually quiet so as to not wake me. I feel happy that they talked Mother into letting me stay at Belmont until the wedding. I do miss Gabby, though. I wonder if the rest of the family will be here early. Then Gabby and I can go exploring in the coconut field before we have to go to the church.

Just then, I hear a knock and come running out of the room. Aunt Allie opens the front door. Gabby is standing there.

"Gabby!" I yell and run to him. "How you get here?"

"We pick a lot of limes while you sick. A truck was bringing them to the lime factory this morning so I ask Dad if I could come. Mom's bringing my clothes for the wedding later."

I grab his hand and pull him downstairs, calling to La-La, "Gabby's here. He'll need food too."

Then we take off out the door that leads to the wash house.

"Where we going?"

Gabby doesn't know Belmont as well as I do.

"The stream," I tell him. "To catch crayfish."

I lead him to the back of the wash house where the stream gently gurgles. The water is cascading from the hill and beckons me to explore.

"You know we shouldn't do this," Gabby says, "not on Aunt Marlene's big day."

He's probably right, but I can't resist the lure. We move forward until we are standing on the bank of the ravine watching the water rush past. Quickly we follow the stream past the wash house, through some of the coconut trees. Soon we come to the pond where the water collects. From there it flows to the sea at the bottom of our land.

"A crayfish!" I exclaim, pointing. "It'll make a nice meal for La-La."

I begin to slide down the bank and bend over to grab the crayfish.

"You sure you want to do that?" Gabby calls out.

Before I can answer, I lose my balance and fall headfirst into the stream. It carries me into a pond where it's too deep for me to stand. In a panic, I splash my hands frantically as my scrawny little body sinks underwater. My feet touch the bed of the stream and I use them to push myself up, gasping for air. I'm soon back on the bottom again, kicking my feet, my lungs screaming for air. My head pops up out of the water. My mouth explodes.

"Help, Gabby!"

Down I go yet again with my hands flailing wildly. Suddenly, I feel small hands around my waist pushing me up. The motion slowly carries me to the far side. I crawl up the bank by grabbing the root of a tree. Gabby pops up below me. Soaking wet, we try to figure out how to get back on the other side of the stream.

"We can go down to the sea and cross there," I suggest.

Gabby shakes his head. "If the tide is high, it'll be too deep there too."

"We can cross before the deep part," I say.

"What if we slip?"

Gabby is cautious by nature. I look around for another way to get home. Finally, we make our way up to the road where the water is very shallow. Soon we're back at the house, explaining to Aunt Clara that we had an accident. She strips off our wet clothes and wraps towels around us. Then we sit quietly while we wait for Gabby's clothes to arrive so we can dress for the wedding. La-La comes upstairs with two bowls of porridge. She puts them in front of us and shakes her head.

"Child, your name is TROUBLE," she says, giving me a piercing look.

"Me too, La-La?" Gabby asks as he likes to be included in everything.

"You all know better," she says.

She's looking at both of us, but I know she's really speaking to me. After a while, Aunt Marlene comes upstairs. She takes one look at us and gasps.

"Why are you wearing towels?" Her face shows her frustration. Her little brothers are not supposed to wear towels on her "perfect" day.

"We had an accident this morning." I make sure my voice is very calm.

"Where?"

I must think fast. It won't do to tell her where we really were. But before I can come up with a harmless response, Gabby pipes up:

"In the ravine."

Aunt Marlene's fists fly to her hips. "What were you doing near the ravine? You know the rules. Now you know why. Come, let's take these towels off. You can wear your pajamas until after lunch. The wedding's not until four o'clock."

Gabby raises his hand. "My pajamas not here."

"Take one of his," she says, pointing at me. Then she admonishes, "You both need to stay clean until the wedding is over, understood? No more going outside, no more exploring. You can colour until lunch. Do you think you can survive until lunch?"

"If we have to," I mutter.

A few minutes later Aunt Allie comes upstairs and exclaims, "How come you two are in your pajamas? You should go out and play."

"But Aunt Marlene won't be happy. She told us to stay right here until lunch."

"Nonsense. Children need fresh air," she says in the tone she uses when she is wearing her nurse's uniform. "Especially you, Vunga. You should be outside after being cooped up for so long."

Aunt Allie leads us to the side door and down the path to where Bobby the German Shepherd is lying in the shade of the fern hedge. We kneel down and pat the dog on his head. After a while Bobby decides to lie down under the ferns, where we join him. When I hear a vehicle pull up in front of the house, I jump up and dash up the path, and Gabby runs after me. My family piles out of the rented wagon and we all go in to lunch. Aunt Marlene is doing wedding stuff so she's not there to notice the smudges of dirt on our knees and faces.

After we stuff ourselves, La-La hurries us to the wash house where we are sponged, dried, and helped into our wedding clothes. These consist of brand-new short pants and long-sleeved white shirts with ruffles down the front and around the collar and cuffs. When we're ready, La-La brings us to the living room and explains that from this moment on we are in her care, and there will be no playing or running around until we leave for the church at three o'clock.

It's agony just sitting here with La-La humming hymns the whole time. I can hear my sisters helping each other and Mother get dressed in their fancy clothes. Finally, a horn sounds. Dad comes into the living room and calls everyone in to pray before we all pile into the cars that will bring us to the church for the "perfect" wedding.

Everything runs smoothly until just before the wedding procession. We're all lined up waiting for the Wedding March to begin when Gabby mutters, "Oh, oh!"

"What?" Aunt Marlene asks anxiously.

"The ring," cries Gabby. "It's not on the cushion."

"Vunga, put down the veil and run to the altar and get the best man. Quick," Auntie orders.

Realizing the urgency, I run full tilt to the front of the church and call out, "Who's the best man?"

A slim man steps forward. I grab his hand and pull him as fast as I can past the whispering guests to the back of the church.

Aunt Marlene asks him, "Roscoe, where's the ring?"

He pulls out his wallet and fumbles through it.

"The ring must have fallen out when I took out that list to give to the pastor."

He retraces his steps, then bends down and peers underneath the pulpit area.

"Found it!" he calls.

But no matter how hard he stretches his arm, he can't reach the ring. He turns to me.

"I think you're thin enough to crawl under there," he says. "Be a good lad and give it a try."

I drop to my knees without hesitation. It's my chance to save Aunt Marlene's perfect day. I see the ring wedged in a far corner. Lying on my stomach, I wriggle forward until I can finally reach it. I am slowly inching my way out when my pants catch on something.

"I'm stuck!" I yell.

Within seconds, I feel strong hands gripping both my ankles and pulling me out. At the same time, I hear something rip. As soon as I'm free, I run toward the back of the church to take up my position so the ceremony can begin. There is a roar of laughter from the guests as my shorts slide down to my knees.

I can see from Aunt Marlene's face that her "perfect" day just got a little less perfect.

"My Lord, child!" Mother exclaims as she rushes toward me.

She picks me up and carries me to the foyer. There, she sets me down and checks the damage to my pants. The button and the zipper are completely destroyed. She reaches into her purse, brings out safety pins, and fastens my pants around my waist. Then she brushes the dirt from my clothes.

"Now, dear, try to control yourself," she says and helps me gather up the train to hold during the ceremony.

The organ strikes up the Wedding March. With Gabby leading, we slowly make our way to where the groom and the pastor are waiting for the bride. The ring bearer and the flower girls take their places. No one tells me where to go, so I sit down on the floor while the ceremony continues. I'm so proud that I didn't make any mistakes to embarrass Aunt Marlene. I can hear little whispers and some snickering. I look around, but I don't see anything weird or funny.

When the music starts up again, I jump to my feet, grab the corners of the veil, and wait until the bride and the groom turn and begin walking toward me. I quickly step to one side of the aisle, but Aunt Marlene waves frantically for me to move to the other side. I hurry across the aisle just as Gabby comes running to take his place in front of them. His head catches in the train. We lose our balance and tumble down, all wrapped up in the veil, which falls off the bride's head. Gabby quickly unwraps himself from the train and then helps me free myself.

"Here, Auntie," he says as he calmly hands her the part of the veil that goes on her head.

She puts it back in place with tears streaming down her face. Gabby holds one side of the train and I the other. At least I can stop worrying about ruining her "perfect" day. I can't imagine what could still go wrong.

We cross the street to the hotel for the banquet. Gabby turns to me and smiles.

"We did good today. I'm starving."

"Me too. La-La said there's always lots of stuff going on before they serve the food," I tell him. "Are you thinking what I'm thinking?"

Gabby grabs my hand and we run toward the kitchen. It is easy to find. We simply go in the opposite direction of the people in uniform carrying trays and pitchers. In no time at all, we come upon four trolleys of food. Everything smells delicious. There's callaloo soup and curried chicken and rice and beans. We settle on the curried chicken, choosing the drumsticks because there are no forks in sight. We graze until a server walks up to us.

"What's going on here?" he queries.

"It's my sister's wedding and we're very hungry," I explain as we wipe our hands on our white shirts and use our sleeves to clean our faces.

"In that case, come with me," he says.

The server escorts us to the banquet room where we point out Mother. She calmly walks over to us.

"Madam, I believe these two are yours," the server says and walks away.

She puts her hands on our shoulders and marches us to the head table.

"You realize that curry will never come out of your shirts," she says.

Right now, curry stains are the farthest thing from my mind. There's a look of sheer horror on Aunt Marlene's face and tears are once again streaming down her cheeks. Before we can apologize, her new husband is on his feet, taking her in his arms.

"Sweetheart, I love you. I love everything about you. Nothing else matters, not the ripped pants or the curried shirts. The important thing is that we're now a family."

As Bertrand takes out a handkerchief and wipes the tears from her eyes, I know that it doesn't matter if the day wasn't perfect after all. The important thing is that Aunt Marlene has married the perfect man.

7

BELMONT MISCHIEF

By the time our parents are ready to take us home after Aunt Marlene's big wedding, all thoughts of punishment have vanished from my mind and I'm ready for the next adventure. One of the good things about being a child is there's no time to worry about anything for very long.

"You know what we should do when we get home?" I ask Gabby. Already he looks wary. Nevertheless, I forge ahead. "We could go sliding down the hill by the road that goes past the spring."

"You mean that really long road that goes down to the coconut trees?"

"Yeah!" Just the thought of it makes me tingle all over. "We'll go very fast," I say with a gleam in my eyes.

Gabby may be cautious, but he loves sliding.

"Boys, the cars are here," Dad calls out.

He directs us to the one where Aunt Clara and Aunt Allie are standing. Aunt Clara is holding a small overnight bag that probably has our pajamas and some play clothes. I look at Gabby and he looks at me and our faces break out in glee. We can go sliding any time, but we rarely have the opportunity to explore the Belmont property since I'm usually bedridden with fever when I'm there.

"Come on, boys, join me in the back," says Aunt Clara.

We quickly hop in, one on each side of her.

"Auntie, why we coming with you?" I want to know.

"Because there's no room in the other car. Besides, Mom and Dad want to rest up a bit. We'll bring you back to Calivigny tomorrow."

I can hardly wait to get to the house in Belmont. It's the first time I'll be there when I'm not sick.

The next morning, I wake up and pop out of bed.

"Gabby," I whisper in his ear.

"Huh!" He shoots upright.

"Come."

He crawls out of bed, rubbing his eyes. We put on our play clothes and sneak out of the room. I take his hand and walk toward the stairs. As we pass the banister, I give it a little pat and whisper, "Someday I'll slide on you."

Sliding down the Belmont banister is strictly forbidden.

"Let's see what we can find in the wash house," I suggest.

But when we get there, we find the door to the wash house locked. I look around for something else to do. My eyes alight on the mango tree up on the hill across the road. I'm starving. La-La hasn't gotten up to make our breakfast yet. Gabby must be hungry too. I look back at the house to make sure no one is watching us. Calivigny and Belmont roads are both very busy.

"We can get some mangoes," I suggest.

"Best we go home," Gabby says.

"But I want to get some mangoes."

So, we stand there watching one bus after another going toward town, then a car, then a truck. As soon as it passes, I dash into the street. Horns honk and brakes screech but I make it to the other side.

"Watch out!" Gabby yells.

Turning, I realize I'm right in the path of a bicycle coming down the road.

I freeze on the spot. The man on the bike swerves sharply, careening up a steep slope and tumbling back down on top of me.

"Boy, you crazy?" the man hollers as he struggles to get up.

"Sorry, sir," I cry through my tears, "I didn't see you coming."

"Where do you live?"

"There, sir," I reply, pointing to the Belmont house.

Seeing the big man hovering over me, Gabby dashes across the road.

"Leave my brother alone!" he screams.

The man looks at me sternly. "Take me to your parents."

I know better than to argue with an adult, or even look him in the face. We wait until the road is clear, then walk across with Gabby between us. When we arrive at the house, the man demands, "Bring your parents out here."

Luckily, my parents are at Calivigny. Dad, especially, would not be pleased about this. I run inside and return in a few minutes with La-La in tow. The man looks at her and speaks in a gruff voice.

"Is this boy yours?"

"Why you ask?"

"We just had an accident on the road."

"On the road? He and you in an accident?"

"Yes. I'm coasting down the hill on my bike and he run out from behind a big truck. I swerve to miss him but the bike and I fall back on him."

"Oh! So, you and the bike hit *him*." La-La turns to me and asks, "Did you stop when you see the bicycle?"

"Yes. I stop and he and the bike knock me down."

La-La straightens up and gives the man *the look*. With her fists digging into her hips, she looks positively fierce, like a lioness protecting her young. The man shrivels up like a mouse in front of a cobra. Without a further word, he mounts his bicycle and rides off toward town.

La-La then turns her wrath on me. "Child, you goin' be the death of me. Now get inside."

We follow her into the house, then go to our bedroom.

As soon as we hear La-La in the kitchen, I take Gabby's hand and lead him outside to where Bobby the dog is resting by his water bowl. I help Gabby get on the dog's back and lead them about the yard with Gabby clinging to Bobby's neck. We're both laughing with the thrill of our new experience when a cat dashes out from behind the fence. Bobby takes off in hot pursuit with Gabby hanging onto his neck.

"Stop, Bobby, stop!" I yell as I run after them.

The dog is barking and Gabby is bawling as he bounces up and down like a rodeo rider. The cat runs along the hedge that separates the Belmont yard from the neighbour's property, and without any warning, disappears into it. Bobby comes to an abrupt halt, flinging Gabby into the hedge. Running hard to keep up with the cat and the dog, I run right into Bobby and fall onto his back. This makes him take off again, running circles around the yard.

"Stop, Bobby! Whoa!" I shout, still clinging to his neck.

Gabby stands by the hedge, brushing twigs and leaves off his clothes. I can hear him calling, "Stop, Bobby, stop . . ."

Suddenly, La-La appears out of nowhere. Bobby takes one look at her, dumps me at her feet, and trots off to his favourite shady spot by the hedge.

She picks me up, brushes me off, and leads me into the house. Gabby follows on our heels.

"Now you two go put on some clean clothes, then come down to breakfast," she orders.

On the way upstairs, I stop and give the banister a friendly pat. Maybe we can sneak some sliding in before we have to go back to Calivigny.

8

POLLY THE SQUEALER

As boys living on a small island, Gabby and I have no idea what's happening in other parts of the world. Of course, this is well before the days of television and sophisticated digital games, and so we go about playing with whatever we can get our eager little hands on. Mainly, we make mischief to keep ourselves busy. For respite, our parents often send us to the house in Belmont to stay with Aunt Allie and Aunt Clara, who manages the big store in town. Since they both work, they in turn request the services of the Calivigny nanny.

When we wake up the next morning, La-La enters the bedroom, humming away.

"Well, well," she says laughingly. "Look what the cat bring!"

"La-La, you staying with us?" I blurt out.

"Yes, baby, until Ma'am come for you."

Since Mother is very busy with her shop, we could be at Belmont for some time. I smile gleefully.

"Awk, awk!"

"What's that sound?" Gabby asks.

"Miss Clara say it's a parrot. His name is Polly and he belongs to a patient of Miss Allie's. She promised the man she look after it while he's in the hospital."

I jump out of bed. "Let's go and see it."

La-La shakes her head. "No child, that's why me here. To keep the bird safe and you out of trouble."

"Why can't we see the parrot?" I ask, giving La-La my fiercest scowl.

"Because you goin' to read and write so the poor bird have peace."

"I think it squawks because it's lonely," I argue.

"Now is time for breakfast."

We follow her into the dining room. We usually only eat in the dining room on Sunday.

"This is for when we come from church, La-La. Every other day we sit downstairs in the kitchen."

"But the parrot is downstairs and you not to play with it."

Gabby's head droops.

"Don't worry," I say as I wink at him. "Aunt Clara will let us play with it."

We devour the salt fish cakes and bakes La-La sets before us. After breakfast she brings our books to the table and gets us to read for a time. Then she has us write on our slates.

"When you done, you can play in the yard by the kitchen window," she says, then adds, "Nowhere else, cause me want to see you."

We run out to the yard where Bobby is lying in the shade. He wags his tail and slowly gets up. We begin to walk around the yard with him. I give Gabby my *ready for adventure* look and he smiles.

"One of us can walk Bobby and the other can go through that door," I say, pointing at the side entrance that leads to the downstairs rooms and, of course, the birdcage.

"You sure that's a good idea?" he asks. As usual, Gabby has misgivings.

"Sure," I say in a big, bold voice. "I'll go in first and you keep walking Bobby, and then we'll switch."

I open the door slowly and slide inside, closing it behind me. I walk toward where the everyday table is. As I turn the corner to enter the big room next to the kitchen, the parrot begins squawking and flapping about in his cage, sounding really angry. La-La comes rushing out of the kitchen.

"Out of here," she shouts. "Right now!"

I stand there as if glued to the floor. La-La has never shouted like that before. She grabs a towel from the drying rack and wraps it around the cage. As the bird calms down, so does La-La. My feet unfreeze and I quietly go back out to the yard.

"It didn't work, huh?" Gabby asks.

I shake my head. "I guess we'll have to wait until Aunt Allie comes home."

Aunt Allie arrives shortly after Aunt Clara. La-La calls us to supper and we all walk down to where the parrot is. Happily, the bird doesn't throw another fit when he sees me. I'm thankful when he greets Aunt Allie.

"Allie home," he says. "Awk, awk! Allie home."

"Yes, Polly, I'm home," Auntie confirms. "You have a good day?"

"Polly happy. Awk, awk! Polly happy."

We all sit down to supper, which consists of a large grouper fish served with eddoes, white yam, sweet potatoes, and green peas. Our aunts chat about Kyle, Aunt Clara's new boyfriend. It's always big news when one of our sisters has a serious beau. *Serious* means maybe we'll get a new uncle. The important thing is not to let Dad know about him too soon. Dad has a habit of chasing away any man that shows an interest in my sisters.

Gabby and I, bored, consume the meal as quickly as we can.

"Can I take Polly out of his cage?" I ask hopefully.

"Why?" Aunt Allie gives me her *what are you up to?* look.

"So he can run about the house like us."

Gabby looks doubtful. Maybe he's even a little afraid. "Isn't it bedtime?" he pipes up.

Aunt Clara checks her watch. "Oh, yes," she says, "both of you off to bed now. No dawdling."

I turn to my little brother on the way to our bedroom. "Why you say that?" I ask. "Maybe she would say yes."

"I see her eyes," he answers. "They say no."

"You always see trouble," I say accusingly. "Maybe you afraid."

Before Gabby can protest, La-La and our older sisters come and tuck us in.

After they leave, I ask, "So how'll we be in trouble if we play with Polly?"

"He can fly," Gabby explains, "and the windows are open to get fresh air. If we let him out of the cage, we done for."

As usual, the voice of reason puts an end to any fanciful talk. Still, long after Gabby drops off to sleep, I think about how grand it would be to walk around the house with Polly on my shoulder. I am so excited thinking about this, I can't sleep. Finally, I shake Gabby awake and we head downstairs. Polly is also awake.

"Maybe he wants to play too," I say to Gabby.

"Maybe not."

I can tell by the hesitation in his voice that Gabby isn't convinced.

"Only one way to find out," I decide.

I pull a chair under the cage, climb up, and open the door. "Polly, come play with us."

The bird just stands there. He looks at me, then at my brother. I get down off the chair and move away from the cage. Polly turns and walks to the back of the cage, then he runs through the open door. To our delight, he flies across the room and lands on the kitchen table.

"Pretty Polly, let's play," I plead with him as I walk toward the bird.

When I am almost an arm's length away, he takes off.

"Gabby, come help me catch Polly," I yell as I chase the bird.

"Stop yelling," Gabby cautions. "You going to wake up La-La and the aunties."

I stop and listen, terrified that Aunt Clara, Aunt Allie, or La-La has heard all the commotion, but all is quiet upstairs.

"Okay, let's go," I whisper.

We make it to the top of the stairs in time to see Polly land on the back of the sofa, facing an open window. I walk along the wall on the left side of the sofa and signal to Gabby to approach the bird from the other side.

"Now!" I call out as we reach the corners, but Polly takes off across the living room.

We dash after him as he heads toward the bedrooms. All the doors are closed, including the one to the concrete steps leading outside. When Polly sees there's no escape, he begins to squawk loudly. One of the bedroom doors swings open just as we arrive in front of it. The parrot flies through the open door and smack into Aunt Allie's face, knocking her to the floor. La-La and Aunt Clara come running into the room, brushing both of us aside. Aunt Clara kneels down beside Aunt Allie, who is laughing so hard she can hardly speak.

La-La plants herself before Gabby and me, fists on her hips, and chides, "You know now why you don't supposed to play with parrots?"

"The bird is all right," I plead my case.

"And your sister?"

"I'm okay," Aunt Allie says, smiling at us, "just some scratches on my face. Polly got a little scared, that's all."

La-La takes my chin in her right hand.

"Child, you goin' be the death of me yet," she says, shaking her head.

Aunt Clara laughs. Aunt Allie, too. La-La's also laughing as she walks us back to bed.

After breakfast, we head downstairs to see Polly, who is now back in his cage.

"Polly happy. Awk, awk! Polly happy," the bird squawks.

"He always says the same thing," Gabby observes.

"Maybe we can teach him some new words!" Gabby brightens. "Like 'Polly hungry,'" he suggests.

"Or, maybe . . ." I think for a few seconds. "How about this?" I skip around his cage chanting, "Kyle kissed Clara. Kyle kissed Clara."

Gabby giggles and takes my hand and we skip around the cage together.

"Kyle kissed Clara. Kyle kissed Clara."

After a few times, Polly joins in.

"Kyle kissed Clara. Awk, awk! Kyle kissed Clara."

The morning passes quickly. We are having great fun until we hear a car motor. We rush upstairs in time to see Aunt Clara park in the shade and get out of her car. Then a lone figure pedals up the drive. It's Dad on his bike, come to drop off the mangoes in his handlebar basket. Gabby and I look at each other and then at the bird.

"Kyle kissed Clara. Awk, awk! Kyle kissed Clara."

We look out the window. Dad and Aunt Clara are walking up the path.

Gabby and I panic.

"Shh, Polly. Shh." We try to quiet the bird, but he only seems to scream louder.

"Kyle kissed Clara! Awk, awk! Kyle kissed Clara!"

The front door opens. Gabby and I dash out the back and head for the ravine, leaving Aunt Clara and Dad to sort things out. Probably, we'll never see Polly the parrot again.

9

THE CURE

Vunga

When I'm not at the farm in Calivigny or the Belmont house in town, I sometimes stay in Tanteen with Aunt Beth, one of my older cousins. Her house is located where Belmont Road meets Terrell Street. It is just up from the GBSS (Grenada Boys' Secondary School) sports complex. Mom and Dad think I'll keep her busy, seeing as she lives alone and always complains she has nothing to do.

One day, I'm walking home with Aunt Beth as a football match (that's what we call a soccer game in the islands) is in progress. It's obvious the boys are having lots of fun.

"Can I watch the game?" I ask Aunt Beth.

"If you stay in the yard."

After a little time passes, I pick out one of the smallest boys and pretend it's me playing instead of him. I follow his every move and feel his excitement. I try to do exactly what he's doing. I even call out, "Pass it to me, pass it to me!"

Auntie comes running outside. "Vunga, what's all the racket?"

"I'm just pretending. It's so much fun."

"Please be careful, you know how easily you get sick."

"I'm okay."

She frowns and goes inside. I continue running after my imaginary ball.

After the game I go into the house. Aunt Beth takes one look at me and puts her hand on my forehead.

"My goodness, you're burning hot. Were you running around with those boys? We'd better get you into a cool bath right away. Didn't I say to just *watch* from the yard?"

"But I wasn't running with the boys. I only *pretended* to play the game," I plead my case as I have no intention of being immersed in a tub of cold water. "It was such fun. I really felt like I was playing."

"Well, drink a glass of water and sit down until supper."

She's right, of course. I do feel tired and hot, so I reach for a glass of water to take with me to the pantry as I watch Auntie cook supper. After we eat the delicious dry-peas soup with clic-clic dumplings and slices of green plantain, Aunt Beth puts me to bed.

In the morning, I wake to birds singing outside my window. I'm just about to leave for school when my big brother Pounda comes to the door.

"No school for you today," he says. "We're going to meet a doctor from far away. Mother and Dad took the bus this morning and will meet us at the hospital. We'll ride up there on my bike."

He's piqued my curiosity. It's not often I get to see people who weren't born on the island. "What's happening?"

"Somebody made a new medicine that can make you feel good all the time."

My eyes open wide and my face lights up with glee.

"They're only testing it now, but they think there's a good chance it'll work."

I start thinking of all the things I could do if that nasty malaria goes away. It makes the ride go really fast. When we arrive at the hospital waiting room, Dad takes my hand and walks me up to the big desk.

"Welcome, young man," the lady behind the desk says. "Thank you for helping us test this new medicine. Today you'll meet a very important doctor. He came all the way from Canada to help you get better. Is that okay with you?"

"Yes ma'am," I say, holding my head down as is the custom when speaking to our elders.

She invites me to take a seat in the adjoining alcove. My parents are to stay in the waiting room. Dad gives me his *be brave, son* nod. Mother gives me her *you better sit quietly or else* look.

"Mind you stay seated in that chair," she says.

I sit down as instructed and take a quick look around. There's nothing interesting to see or do, so I reach into my pocket and pull out my top. I rewind the twine real tight and toss it across the floor, giving the cord a sharp jerk. At that precise moment, a nurse walks into the alcove. She steps on my top and goes flying, landing with her back on the floor and her legs up in the air. A folder flies out of her hand, scattering papers everywhere. She gets up, collects herself and her papers, and as if nothing happened, she calmly turns to me and queries, "Are you the volunteer for the medicine test?"

I'm too scared to answer. I sit there contemplating the consequence of my actions. I imagine sitting in a corner of a room for days on end with Gabby bringing my meals and walking away without saying a word, or practising writing with my right hand for three hours every day after school. (Mother made sure my slate came to Tanteen with me.)

My thoughts break when a soft hand touches my face and a tender voice says, "You must be the young master, right?"

"Yes, ma'am."

"Would you come with me, please?"

I glance into the big waiting room. Mother and Dad are both standing at the desk up front, filling out forms. They missed the whole incident with the top. My knees are almost shaking with relief.

The nurse leads me into a small room where a big man is sitting behind a desk. She takes me to a gurney behind a screen and helps me undress and put on a white gown. I can hear the doctor explaining about the program, which is sponsored by UNICEF. After a few minutes, the talking stops and the doctor comes in to see me. He tells me that if it works, the medicine will cure me and prevent me from getting malaria again. He gives me an injection.

"I want to thank you for being so brave and allowing us to test this medicine on you. It will save many lives if it works."

He gives me a piece of gauze to hold on the site where the needle went in, then tells me to go join my parents in the waiting room. As I'm leaving his office, I notice my top on his desk.

I try to look at it without looking too hard. The doctor doesn't say anything, but I can feel him watching me. Our eyes meet. Then we both look at the top.

"I suppose you would like this back, young man." His voice is kind but firm.

I nod.

"Well," he says, "this top almost hurt a very important person. Would you agree?"

My heart sinks as the image of the nurse lying on the floor pops into my head. I nod. I'm trying very hard to be brave, but tears are spouting out of my eyes.

"It's my only toy," I tell him. "My brother Slingshot made it for me."

"Well, tell your brother I admire his carving skills."

"Yes, sir."

The doctor gets up from his desk. I feel an arm around my shoulder.

"I know you're a good boy," he says, "but try and be more careful. When I was your age, I was in trouble often. I know just how you feel."

He smiles and hands me my top. My heart jumps with joy. I scamper off to find my parents. To my surprise, Gabby is standing next to Auntie Clara. His face lights up like a full moon at night.

"Auntie brought me here from Calivigny to see if I could get the medicine too. I'll be staying with you and Aunt Beth until Sunday."

Gabby—here in Tanteen for a whole week! I grab his hand and we both jump up and down. Aunt Allie hurries toward us, wagging her finger.

"Shush," she says. "There are a lot of sick people in this hospital."

Mother guides us to a corner of the room, where she squats down and cautions:

"I don't want to hear that you boys are giving Aunt Beth any trouble. Understand?"

Gabby and I nod sagely. I don't think Mother notices our fingers crossed behind our backs.

10

HUNTING THE GUNDY CRAB

For the first time since returning home to the farm, I wake up without being called. Aunt Clara brought us back to Calivigny last night. She said Aunt Beth needed a rest. Strength is coursing through my scrawny frame with thoughts of adventure racing around my brain. Gabby is standing at the door grinning. His eyes sparkle with readiness.

"It's a great day for an adventure," he announces, doing his mind-reading thing again.

I'm up and dressed in no time at all. We run down to the kitchen. La-La's away so Mother is preparing breakfast.

"My, my, sons, what's all the excitement?" she asks.

"We're happy, Mom. We're together with our family," I explain.

I think but do not say out loud: *Our huge, wonderful family with so many possibilities for adventure.* Mother doesn't appreciate adventure the same way we do.

"Why don't the two of you go watch your brothers milk the cows?" she suggests.

We head down the path to learn how to milk the cattle, skipping all the way. On the way home after the milking, Slingshot asks, "You ever go hunting for crabs, Vunga?"

"Vunga likes the idea of hunting crabs," Gabby pipes up. Gabby's mind-reading thing is getting out of hand. I feel the need to assert myself.

"Not just any crab," I tell them. "I think we should try to catch the Gundy Crab."

"What you talking about?" Gabby inquires.

"The monster crab that lives in that giant hole near the well," I shoot back.

Slingshot snorts. "Good luck with that."

"You mean next to the cocoa and avocado trees in the bottom land?" Gabby confirms.

"It's the crab to beat all crabs," I assure him.

"So how we going to catch it?"

"With a trap," I tell him. "I saw one on a pile of stuff in the root cellar."

Slingshot laughs. "That old thing? It's so rotten it can't even hold a mouse, much less a big crab. That's why it's on the reject pile. Count me out," he says as we approach the kitchen. "I got girls to meet."

I turn to Gabby. "You with me?" I ask hopefully.

"Of course, we're a team," Gabby replies, then voices his concern. "We have wood and a saw and a hammer and nails?"

"I don't know where to find wood," I admit, "but Dad has lots of tools in a corner under the house."

"I think there's some boards under the shop."

"If worse comes to worst we can always take some wood from the outhouse," I tell Gabby.

"What! You crazy?" he asks, his eyes big like saucers. "Dad'll kill us for sure."

When Gabby gets alarmed, it's usually wise to abandon a plan and stick to a safer idea.

"Then let's go see what we can find around here," I say.

We quietly pass in front of the kitchen. We are especially careful to walk silently toward the storage space. It's under this back part of the house that Mother can see if she happens to look up, so we tiptoe until we reach the door and are safe from her sharp eyes. Gabby lights an oil lamp and we scamper into the storage area, where we find all Dad's tools.

I know Gabby likes to sort through things, so I ask him to pick the best tools while I look for boards. As I'm looking at the nice timber stored on the back wall, it occurs to me that it might be best to ask Dad which boards he doesn't really need. Acting on this thought, I rejoin Gabby, who's sucking wet sugar from a ladle. My eyes are as large as saucers as my hands fly up and squeeze the sides of my head in an effort to hold back the explosion pounding to escape from my wide-open mouth.

"What?" Gabby asks.

"Dad will kill us if he finds out we eat his wet sugar," I say in a loud whisper. "That's what!"

I take the ladle from him and help him lick it until all the sugar is gone. Then I put the ladle on its holder and we head back outside.

"Maybe Dad knows where we can get some old wood," Gabby suggests.

"Or Uncle Jack," I say. "He should know where we can get boards for free. His place is full of stuff he finds all over the place."

We decide to ask him on Sunday when he comes for lunch after church. On Saturday, Gabby and I get the old trap out of the junk heap and examine it. We need to know just how to fix it so we can catch the famous Gundy Crab. We sit on the side of the slope in the shade of a banana tree. It's nice and quiet. Gabby is busy drawing a trap on his slate. Dad, our sisters, and our older brothers are in town. Mom's in the shop talking with customers. Our two little brothers are sliding down the hill on coconut branches between where we're sitting and the pigpen.

I lie back on the soft blanket of grass and let the breeze from the lagoon waft over me. How wonderful it is to be back on the farm where there's always something interesting and fun to do.

Gundy Crab, you better watch out!

Monday afternoon, Gabby and I hurry to pick up the board and nails at Uncle Jack's farm. All the way back we talk about the size of the crab and the best way to get it to go into the trap.

"After all, the Gundy Crab has lived a very long time. That means it's very smart," Gabby says sagely.

"True," I agree. "We need the best bait. Maybe peas or corn."

"Uh-uh," Gabby says, shaking his head. "Lolli have a friend whose brother traps crabs. She say he use mango or golden apple or sugarcane."

I leap to my feet.

"You start making the trap and I'll go up by the road and pick some mangoes."

I walk up the hill to the mango tree that clings perilously to the jagged, rocky terrain. Its roots are gnarled and get buffeted by torrents of water when it rains. Soon I return with four very ripe fruit and gleefully join Gabby at the mill. Naturally, we eat one before starting our task of building a great trap.

By the time we finish making the trap, it's time to bring the cows in from the pasture. Pounda and Slingshot are already heading toward the spring. We help our brothers water the animals then bring them up to their straw beds near the sugar mill. Afterwards, Gabby and I fetch the trap and hurry to the Gundy Crab's hole before he comes out to wander about for food. By the time we reach the well, the sun is sinking in the west.

We put the mango bait on the trigger inside the trap and set up trap right in front of the hole. The next morning I shake Gabby awake before daybreak. I grab a crocus bag from the storage room and we race down to the trap. The water is running in the little stream past the well. We hear a frog grunting as we approach the trap. Gabby grabs my hand.

"You afraid?" I whisper.

"It's really dark. You hear the twig snap?"

"Uh-huh!" I say, then try to distract him by telling him the plan. "Okay, you hold the trap over the mouth of the bag and ease it down so the crab has to drop into it. When I say *now*, pull the trap door wide open. Got it?"

"Yeah, but where's the crab?"

"It's not there?"

"No."

"Knock the back of the trap hard to scare it out," I tell him.

We're both nervous. I close the mouth of the bag as Gabby drops the trap and lights a match. He lifts the trap door to look for the crab.

"No crab in here," he says. "No bait neither. You feel in the bag. It must be in there."

I pat the bag all over and shake my head. "There's no crab. No nothing. To think a stupid crab outsmarted me," comes my solemn declaration.

How that feeling of failure presses against my shattered pride!

"The Gundy Crab isn't stupid," Gabby says. "That's why nobody can catch him."

As we walk back to the house, a thought crosses my mind. "I know how the crab escaped. The Gundy Crab is even bigger than we thought. And this crab is so clever it can reach into the trap with its giant claw and grab the bait while it holds the trapdoor open with its small claw."

"Yeah, so we need a bigger trap."

"Yeah! We'll make a trap twice the size of the other one. Then we get him for sure."

"We going to build the biggest trap ever," we chant as we run up the path to the kitchen for breakfast.

I am so excited that breakfast and the fieldwork and lunch just fly by until it's time to make the giant trap.

"Soon we'll conquer the king of the bottom land—Mr. Gundy Crab," I boast to Gabby.

"Off to the hunt, trusty warriors," we shout as we bolt down the hill toward the sugar mill.

We take a shortcut, passing behind the shop and under the large plum tree where we find a few ripe plums to boost our energy. Upon arriving at the mill, we realize someone has taken the longer boards, leaving just small pieces behind. We are crestfallen.

"Don't worry," I soothe. "I'll be right back."

I sneak up to the house and quietly slip under the shop, ease a long board out, and carry it back to the mill. Gabby is delighted.

"Not a word about where this comes from," I caution.

We measure off each section of the board to twice the length of our first trap. I saw while Gabby holds the board steady. The sawing is hard work and we change places a couple of times. In a few minutes, we have the floor and the sides assembled. Gabby measures two pieces for the back and the trap door and we cut them to length and mount them in place. I take the awl and make a hole in the middle of the backboard. Then we carry the trap to the Gundy Crab's hole. We put the mango bait in the trap then head home to await the morning's conquest.

The night drags slowly as I lie sleepless. I'm up before anyone else and wake Gabby when it's still dark. We sneak down the hill. An owl hoots. I wonder if it knows something about our adventure. It hoots again. Fearful, Gabby grabs my hand.

"It's really dark," he says. "You remember what Mother told us? We can fall and break our bones if we run around in the dark."

"I never heard her say that," I counter and cross my fingers behind my back.

It's spooky out here, but I must get to the trap. Nothing is going to stop me. Just then I feel a drop of rain, and then another, and another. By the time we reach the edge of the cocoa trees, it's pouring. We keep moving, but take shelter under the trees. When we arrive at the well, I grab the bag from under the pepper bush. My heart is pounding and my mouth is bone dry. I can hardly talk. I can hear Gabby's teeth chattering and I know he's scared, too. What if the crab is mad because we tricked him and his big claw is stuck in the trap?

Rumbling thunder rolls across the sky. I open the bag. Slowly, Gabby raises the trap. I stand in front of him holding the bag open and wait for the trap to release the crab. Gabby's hands tremble as he lifts the lid of the trap. Much to our dismay, the trap is empty!

Patow! Patow!

Lightning cuts through the branches of the avocado tree. My knees buckle under me and I tumble to the ground. My head comes to rest next to the crab hole. I feel a swish of wind as the lightning lights up the hole.

"I think I see something flash by," I call out.

Gabby dives forward, plunging his hand into the hole. After a moment, he slowly withdraws it. A very small crab is clinging to his pinky finger with both of its tiny claws.

We stare at the absurd little creature dangling from Gabby's finger and start to laugh, at first with barely audible chuckles, then with huge roars. Our laughter seems to upset the tiny creature because it lets go of the pinky, drops to the ground, and scuttles down the hole in the blink of an eye.

The adventure of the Gundy Crab is over. Or is it?

At breakfast, Dad asks about a missing piece of lumber. It turns out it belongs to Mr. Skinner and is to be delivered to him on Wednesday.

"I saw some wood, some old and some brand new, at the sugar mill," Pounda says.

Slingshot snickers. All eyes turn to look at me as I cower as low as possible into my chair.

VUNGA'S TEENISH YEARS

11

VUNGA'S VERY TALL TAXMAN TALE

It's a drizzly morning so Gabby and I wear shoes to school today. The steady mist of rain creates a cool dampness that makes our clothes cling to our bodies. A truck horn signals that a vehicle is coming around the bend. We move onto the grass to make sure it won't hit us. As it approaches, the driver comes to a stop and yells, "Hop in, I'm going to town."

Gabby and I run up to the truck cab and scramble onto the vacant seat.

"Good morning, sir. Thanks for giving us a ride."

"No problem, boys. Your dad always treats me good."

"You know Daddy!" Gabby says excitedly.

"Of course, we do business together." Then the driver looks at me. "And you must be Vunga."

"Yes, sir. I live with my aunts in town from time to time."

"You," he says, pointing at Gabby, "I see at the farm. How come you don't remember me?"

Gabby thinks for a moment. "You have a mustache now. Your name's Zum-Zum."

"Yeah, that's smart of you to notice." Then he changes the subject. "I keep forgetting to see what happen to the taxman's house. You know anything?"

"No," I answer him, "nothing happening since it burn down."

"But tell me," Zum-Zum continues, "I hear your father had some goings on with the taxman. That right?"

"Yes, sir," I reply. "It happened right before the fire."

Zum-Zum looks at me with big eyes and asks, "What you say?"

"I'll never forget that day."

When I see Zum-Zum is all ears, I can't resist.

One morning a car stops up on the road in front of our house. A voice calls out, "Mr. Beisfil, are you there?"

The voice doesn't sound friendly. No answer from our dad. Mother looks at him with an inquiring eye. Gabby looks at Mother, and then Dad, and then me. I cringe. My little sister crawls under the table.

"Mister, this is an important matter," the voice says. "Can we talk?"

"State your business," Dad shouts back.

"Well, sir, I'm from the tax department. I come to look at your business ledger."

There's no reply. Dad slowly walks up the stairs as if he is very tired. Mother has a worried look on her face. We hear Dad's footsteps going toward the front door. Then *click, click*.

"Oh no!" Mother says. "Your father has the equalizer with him."

"What do you mean *the equalizer*, Mom?" Gabby asks.

"You'll see," I say and demonstrate by pretending to hold a rifle in shooting position and uttering *"Patung, patung!"*

Then we hear the front door open, followed by Dad's voice. "Just why you want to see my books?"

"Well, sir, there seem to be some irregularities in your deductions."

"Are you calling me dishonest?"

Not wanting to miss the action, I shoot past Mother with Gabby right behind me. She grabs our shirts and pulls us back. Dad is holding his three-ought-three double-barrel shotgun at the ready.

"No, no, sir," the taxman pleads in a quivering voice. "We all have respect for you at the office. It's just that some of the labour costs are not quite right. Respectfully, sir."

"Respect? How can you show respect to me by accusing me of . . . what's that you call it?"

"Please, sir, I can get a warrant to take your books, you know. But I would like you to hand them over quietly and save any embarrassment."

"Imba . . . what?" Dad shouts. "You dare to question my labour cost?"

"Please, sir, put the gun away and let us talk about a solution." The taxman sounds real scared.

All the while, Gabby is clinging to my arm. "Don't do it, Daddy! Don't do it!" he's screaming.

I can tell Dad is losing his patience.

"How dare you insult me and my family. You call us thieves. Get off my land right now."

"But sir, you do not understand the severity of your position," the taxman pleads.

"Run, mister, run!" I yell as I yank my arm from Gabby and step in front of my dad. "Please don't shoot him, Dad."

The taxman is frozen where he stands.

"Son, this is between this man and me," Dad explains. "He's insulting the whole family, saying he suspects we are cheating the government of their taxes. From the day my parents brought us here from St. Vincent, we all work hard and honest. When my father died working land to make another man rich, I swore I'll own my own land and defend it with my life. Now, the two of you get in the house so I can conclude this business."

Gabby and I go back to where Mother is standing. Dad turns his attention to the taxman.

"Now, Mr. Taxman, what have you to say about this tax matter?"

The taxman responds to Dad's question slowly, like he is thinking real hard.

"I can understand how your father must have felt having to work land that was not his own. But you own your land, which is commendable. So let us just sit down and go through these files calmly."

"What files?" Dad snaps.

"The files from our office—the papers your lawyer signs on your behalf when he files your tax returns."

"What about them?" Dad asks angrily, losing his patience again.

"Just a few minor errors. You know . . . the amount of people who work for you. Only three of the people who live nearby are on your list of employees. You see the problem, sir?"

"I see no problem. People come from all over to work; some are just passing through. I pay them, they leave, and I never see them again. Isn't that how farms work?"

"There's a feeling at the department that some people make up names to not pay taxes. I only want to verify that all your employees are accounted for."

"Well, that's for you to find out for yourself. For me, I hire people who come and go. You're telling me you want me to find all these hard-working folk who get work where they can find it? How will I be able to do that?"

"If you can't tell us where they are, we will delete their names off your records and reassess how much tax you will pay."

"Is that a threat?"

"No, sir, it's a fact," the taxman says sternly, as if he is speaking to a child.

By this time Dad is fuming. His face is red and his nostrils are flaring.

As the taxman spins around and jumps into his car and starts driving off, a loud crack, like thunder, fills the air. Its tires screeching, the car plunges into the ditch. The taxman gets out and runs all the way home.

Zum-Zum's eyes are wide like saucers. I can tell he believes every word I've said.

"So, has the taxman come back for his car?" he asks.

"Are you kidding? We never heard from him or any other taxman since. A truck hauled the car out of the ditch a few days later."

"I just wish I was there to see the action," Zum-Zum confides.

Gabby rolls his eyes. He always does that when my imagination goes a little wild. Then Zum-Zum lowers his voice.

"You think your dad set the taxman's house on fire?"

Of course, I know my father was away the day of the fire. Still, I smile and ask:

"What do you think?"

Gabby rolls his eyes again.

12

THE GREAT FISHMAN

75

I always wanted to learn how to fish. When I go with my brothers to the lagoon, they always catch fish and I always catch seaweed. It's very frustrating. I do everything they do. I use the same bait they use. But the fish never bite.

Gabby explains the fish do not like my body smell and he puts the bait on my hook for me. After about half an hour, I realize the fish do not like me, period. The next time Fishman comes to our house to sell fish, I will ask him why fish always bite my brothers' bait, but not mine. Not that we get to go fishing much. Our chores keep us plenty busy.

I know Fishman is up really early in the morning. Therefore, I plan to be up when he comes to the house. And how do I know when he's coming to the house? Easy. One day, while Mother is in the shop, I casually comment:

"I feel like eating fried fish. Can we have some soon?"

"Mmm."

That's her *thinking* sound. I'm pretty sure there's an idea running around her head, like: *Vunga is so skinny. If he wants to eat fish, I guess I'd better cook him some.*

"I really like the way you make it," I say in all truthfulness.

"Then this Friday you will have your heart's desire."

I scamper off to make my plans. First, I need to finish milking the cows before five in the morning so I can be there when Fishman arrives. Then I need to find a way to talk to him alone. That's the easy part. The hard part is deciding the right questions to ask him and in what order. I have two really good friends who are almost as smart as I am. Since I have until Friday, we arrange to meet Thursday afternoon.

As usual, I find Tuf-Tuf and Duda under the sugar-apple tree. It's our favourite place to gather because it has a built-in snack. I get right down to business.

"You know Fishman is the best fisherman ever, right?"

"You say," Tuf-Tuf challenges, "but there are lots of others that are really good too."

I do not like to hear my hero belittled. "Come on," I counter, "who you know anywhere that takes each customer's order the day before and brings exactly what they want early the next morning?"

"You mean he really does that all the time?"

"Sure," I boast proudly, enjoying my moment. "Now what do you think are the best questions to ask to get him to show me how to catch fish?"

I toss each of them a sugar-apple, then I take a bite of one.

Duda clears his throat and expounds:

"It's my opinion that this man will not give anyone his secrets. After all, he makes a very good living and still has time to spend most of his day doing things he enjoys. So you need to get him to take you out some time."

Tuf-Tuf scratches his head. "That's all good," he says, "but how do we get Fishman to take Vunga with him?"

By this time, plans are shooting through my brain. I jump up in the air, pumping my fist. "Yes!" I shout. "I got it. I do not ask him. We will get him to ask us."

"You mean we trick him into asking us to go with him to catch fish?" Tuf-Tuf scoffs. "He not stupid, nuh. I know because my mother is cousin to his wife."

Tuf-Tuf is a rotund boy with stubby legs and a full, perpetually happy face. He's noted as being the quickest runner in school, the best footballer, and the best at "liming" in our neighborhood. He also lives across the hill from our farm.

"Your mother know him and you say nothing?" I chide him.

"Me just remember now," Tuf-Tuf argues.

"All right!" I tell him. "You de man. You get your mother to get us to go fishing with him."

"Ah dunno. She don't like me fishing."

I will not be dissuaded. "I really think if we do it right, Tuf-Tuf's mother will get him to do it for us. Let's make a plan. The thing is how to get this man to say he wants us. Tuf-Tuf, does he know you?"

"Yeah, we go to his place and he come to our place once in a while."

Perfect, I think.

"Get your mother to tell him we'd like to help out as it will keep us busy during school break. That'll work, I think."

When my father gets home from town on Saturday, he says:

"I ran into Fishman at the market. He told me he's very impressed that you and your friends offered to help him with his catch. Is that so?"

"Sort of, Dad." It's impossible not to be honest with my dad. He has a kind of built-in fib finder.

"I'm proud of you boys for wanting to help out. Fishman told me he just got a big order from that fancy hotel on Grand Anse Beach and that he'd be happy to have help bringing the order to the truck. He'll talk to your mother. But no fishing, understand?" Dad always wants me to do farm work and schoolwork instead of fishing.

I cross my fingers behind my back. "Yes, sir. No fishing."

"I also saw Duda's father in town. It's okay with him as long as there's no fishing."

"Thanks, Dad."

I dash off to the veranda to plan on how to learn about fishing from Fishman. Tuf-Tuf and Duda are as excited as I am.

On Monday the three of us gather to wait for Fishman to give us our instructions. Upon arrival, he gives us each a small bag of asham (roasted ground corn with salt and black pepper mixed in), one of our favourite snacks.

"I have a special order from the Islander Hotel for a very large swordfish. It has to be delivered by four o'clock on Tuesday afternoon."

"That's tomorrow!" I exclaim.

"Yes. And that's why I want the three of you at Calivigny Harbour by nine in the morning so we can have everything organized. You boys will have to run to the boat when it gets in the shallows and pull it up on the beach. There'll be one of you on each side and one at the bow. I'll push from the back. Is that clear?"

"Yessir," we chorus.

We agree to meet at my house at eight thirty Tuesday morning, then I head home to complete my chores and get the cattle watered and bedded for the night.

The next morning, I'm up at four thirty. I milk the cows with my brothers and help get the cattle to the pastures. Afterward, I wash up and put on old clothes, as we'll be carrying that big fish to the truck.

At breakfast my brothers and sisters are chatting away, but I hear nothing. My mind is all about the giant swordfish. I look at the sun and figure it's near eight. So where are my friends? In a few minutes, I hear someone whistling.

We head down the cliff road to the spring and along the edge of the lagoon to a small peninsula. There the lagoon joins the sea through a small opening between the peninsula and the hill across from it. It isn't long before we are crossing the base of the peninsula to the sea. If the tide is in, we'll have to swim. We make our way through a thicket of brush. After about ten minutes, we are staring at the hill. There are enough rocks to allow us to make it most of the way. We can see the beach ahead, and in the distance beyond the coral reefs, Fishman in his little boat. They look very small. The wind is stronger here. We push onward, jumping from rock to rock, until we are at the beach. We stay there watching Fishman's boat getting smaller and smaller.

After a while, the boat raises a sail and heads into the harbour. Something is wrong. The sail is loose!

"Look!" Duda shouts. "He got something on the line. He's fighting it."

We clap and shout.

"Good. You got him."

"Stick him hard."

"Don't give up."

The ruckus continues as the little boat bobbles in the ocean, still way out from shore. Eventually, Fishman pulls the sail down and rows toward us. He makes it past the reef and it looks as if he has things under control. All of a sudden, we see this large swordfish break the water and dive again. Fishman rows frantically, trying to go as fast as he can. We all stand dumbstruck as the monster fish shoots up high into the air and comes down with its sword heading right for the middle of the boat. We watch, aghast, as the big fish plunges into the boat, expecting the little craft to shatter.

Just as it's going to hit, Fishman grasps the sail and slings it around the creature. With one arm steadying the monster fish and the other holding the top of the oar, Fishman begins to sway the blade back and forth in the sea. Squeaky clunk, squeaky clunk, squeaky clunk. Faster and faster the rhythm goes. We chant:

"Faster, faster, harder, harder. Faster, faster, harder, harder."

We are jumping and chanting as the little boat comes toward us. When it is near the shallows, we run out to meet the great Fishman. I grab the bow, Tuf-Tuf the left side, and Duda the right side. *Crueerrr!* The bottom hits the sand below and the boat stops. My two friends jump into the boat, one on either side of the big fish.

"Pull up, boys. Pull hard," Fishman shouts.

The fish comes flying out of the boat and almost lands on me. I dive right onto the tail and grab the narrow part of the fish just below the main body. Duda and Tuf-Tuf leap out of the boat to make sure the fish does not get away. Fishman hops out and moves the boat along the sand so it will not drift out to sea.

"Okay, boys, we need to keep this fish wet and alive, so go get the buckets in those bushes," he orders. "Remember, it has to be wet all over its body. In the meantime, I have some deliveries to make. I'll be back with the truck."

We walk down to the water and fill our pails. Tuf-Tuf starts dousing the fish's head. When his pail is empty, I start from where he left off. Duda takes over from where I finish. By the time his pail is empty, Tuf-Tuf is back.

Now we know why the fishman is famous for the freshest fish ever. It's about noon when the truck arrives at the beach. Fishman instructs the man riding shotgun.

"Skinner, could you set up the pump to keep the fish wet while the boys eat lunch?"

What a lovely lunch—stewed jacks and lard bread with juicy mangoes after. We wash it all down with cream soda pop, then dash back to the fish.

"Okay, boys. We have some barrels on the truck that need to be filled for the journey. You go back to watering the fish and we'll use the pump for the barrels."

We head off to our duties as Skinner fills the barrel. We sing one of our favourite calypso songs—"All Day, All Night, Marianne"—with Fishman and Skinner joining in. In no time at all, we're ready to load the prize fish onto the truck. Skinner ties a long rope around the swordfish's tail. While he's doing this, Fishman fastens the other end of the rope onto a winch and ratchet. When Skinner waves his hand, Fishman starts turning the handle of the winch and the fish slowly comes closer and closer to the truck. Skinner pulls out a long board from just below the floorboard of the truck. The fish slides up and Fishman secures it to the front of the flatbed. Skinner pushes the board back into its place and heads for the driver's seat. Fishman calls to us.

"Hop on, boys. We're off to the hotel."

We jump onto the flatbed as Fishman starts the little pump, which sends a mist over the six feet of fish. The three of us gather around the greatest fisherman of all time, and I ask the question I've been pondering all morning.

"I wonder if you could tell us something, sir? I have a big problem," I confide. "When I go fishing with my brothers, they always catch fish, but I never even get a bite. Even if somebody else puts the bait on my hook, I don't catch anything. What can I do to catch a fish?"

"That's a tough one," Fishman says. He thinks for a moment. "From my memory, you live in different places, while your brothers always been on the farm. So, it could be that the place you live in now is not where you will live after now. When you find where you are to live all the time, you will catch lots of fish. Don't be discouraged. All things work out."

That is hard to take, but Fishman is the greatest of them all. I respect what he tells me.

"When did you know you'd become a fisherman?"

He smiles and nods.

"When I looked at the sea for the first time. It's a gift. No one had to teach me. I just knew it right from the first time I held a line in my hand. As the good book says, some have one gift and others have other gifts. From what I see, you have another gift. You like to help people. Use it and be happy."

We pull into the hotel service entrance and Skinner backs the truck up to the door. Four men in uniform wheel two carts to the back of the truck and place them side by side. They pull the swordfish across the carts as Fishman enters the kitchen. When he comes out again, he hands us each a bowl of pudding, compliments of the chef. We gobble it down, then Skinner starts up the truck and we three sit in the back on the flatbed.

The journey home is serene. Of course, we're exhausted from our day of hard work. The best part is we all have a great story to share with our families. We drop Duda off at his house. Then Tuf-Tuf and I jump off at my house. Tuf-Tuf sprints down the hill. I dash into the shop, where Mother is sewing.

"Well, what took you so long?" she asks. "You realize you still have chores to do."

Chores? Oops, I forgot. I grab a cutlass and head down the hill to cut fodder for the cattle before they come in for the night. The great adventure is over, but I know I'll remember it forever.

13

ZORRO WANNABES MEET THE SHANGO WOMAN

83

The best thing about being in high school is that Gabby and I are actually allowed to go to town on our own without a parent or older sibling telling us what to do all the way there and back. *Zorro* is playing at the little movie house in town. Of course, we want to go see it with our friends. But in our family, movie-going is a waste of time that only corrupts tender minds.

"They're Satan's tool," Mother will say, wagging her pointing finger in my face.

Cautioning us, Dad will jab both pointing fingers sharply to the ground (we all know the devil lives down there) and say, "Movies are for idle, lazy, good-for-nothing folk."

However, while living with Aunt Beth I developed a taste for movies. She doesn't think they are the work of the devil. Now I'm constantly trying to figure out ways to talk my parents into letting us go to the Saturday matinee.

After many failures, a scheme that might work suddenly dawns on me: *The Mark of Zorro* is about a man who fights a greedy governor in old Spanish California. Maybe I can convince Dad this is an educational film. *Yes!* I smile broadly. I can hardly contain my glee at having come up with such a brilliant plan. Gabby is beside himself with excitement.

We decide to wait for evening to put the plan into action. I smile cunningly as I think: *Dad will be mellow then*. After supper, he always relaxes while I wash his feet. I make sure the water is heated to just the right temperature.

Dad smiles lovingly at me as his feet soak in the warm water, easing the pain of wearing heavy boots all day.

"How was school today?" he asks. I hear by the tone of his voice that he feels very content. It's now or never.

"Fine, Dad," I respond calmly. I pause and then say, "Well, actually, I'm having a little trouble in history class understanding some of the conflicts in Spanish California."

"Is there a school book on it?" he asks.

I didn't expect that. After all, Dad has very little education as he and his brothers were orphaned young and had to work to support themselves. We read letters and the Bible to him. I ask myself: *What do I say to this?* A new thought flashes into my mind. *Come on, he's just making conversation. That's all.* I slowly let out a relaxing breath before tackling his question.

"Well," I venture, "you remember I have trouble reading, Dad. It's much easier for me to learn when I hear or see things. On Friday after school, there's a film about those events. It's showing at the movie house in town. If I could watch it, I'd get better marks on my final exam."

Dad says nothing. I know this means he's pondering my proposal. As I dry his feet and massage them with baby powder, my heart pounds and sweat beads on my brow. It takes Dad forever to respond.

"I think Saturday afternoon's cheaper than Friday night. But come home right after the film. There's still chores to be done."

I almost bolt right out of my skin. "Yes, sir," I reply.

"I guess Gabby will be going with you, seeing as how he's in that same history class."

"Yes, sir. We'll come right home."

"And I want perfect results on that test."

"Yes, sir."

I have to work hard to contain my excitement. Time crawls at a snail's pace. And sleep? Impossible! Finally, it's four thirty on Saturday morning. Gabby and I throw on our clothes and bound down to the cow pens to milk the cattle. In no time at all, we complete our chores. After a hearty breakfast we're off to town. Walking briskly, we make the four miles to Tanteen in an hour and take a short cut through the high school grounds and the soccer pitch. We quickly come to the entrance to the docks in the harbour. As we turn the corner, we see the Empire Theatre just before the bend on the horseshoe-shaped Carenage.

The water gently laps against the concrete wall that holds the sea back from the road. Trucks and carts jostle for space with bicycles and pedestrians along the harbour wharfs. There's excitement in the air.

Being early, we have time to savour the wares of street vendors near the movie house. The smells of spiced black pudding, fish cake, and ripe plantain frying in large pans tantalize our palates. Gabby reads out loud the choices of seats and the prices. *Balcony, house, pit.* Since this could be the last time we ever get to see a movie, we decide to get the best seats. That means balcony, where staff will serve us treats during the show.

We get into the line forming at the ticket window. I check to see if any of our friends are in the line. Six people back, I see a classmate in a khaki shirt with a turned-up collar. His pants are khaki too. He dresses like this because he wants to be a soldier and fight for the Empire in exotic places when he grows up. He's tall and muscular with a head shaped like a rugby ball. Thus, his nickname.

"Hey, Keel-Head!"

"Vunga! What you doing here?" he shouts back in country slang. "I never seen you at the movies before."

"True, man, it's my first time here, but I already been in Tanteen. Gabby too."

"What ticket you going to buy?"

"Balcony, man, for the free food."

"Ha! It's just asham and peanuts," he says, but quickly adds, "Okay. We'll do that, Okay?"

I pump the air triumphantly with my fist. "Okay! We going to raise hell up there, man!"

When we enter the theatre, an usher looks at our tickets and points to a set of stairs. We bound up the steps two at a time. Upon reaching the balcony, we look at the upholstered seats. They are all leather, clean and inviting. We gaze at them for a few seconds and Keel-Head's eyes open very wide. His lips part until his mouth is a gaping hole and he whispers, "Wow, man, this is class. Nothing like the school chairs."

"Those wooden chairs are really hard," Gabby remarks.

"So hard they give me a blister when I have to sit on them all day," I agree.

"Uh-huh." Keel-Head nods. "That's why, from now on, just balcony for me."

We sit in the front row so we can put our feet up on the railing.

"Look down there," Keel-Head explains. "House not so bad. The seats are okay, but all the same height so you will not see the whole screen when people get excited and jump up and down. In de pit, now, you sit on hard benches and look up at the screen. That's really hard on the neck."

"Look who just came in down there!" I exclaim, pointing at a boy wearing short pants and a green short-sleeve shirt. "Hey, Tuf-Tuf!" I shout down to him.

"Crazy man, crazy Vunga. Say, how come you don't come to the movie more?" he calls back. "What you doing up there? You going to get nosebleed, you know."

"You jealous, nuh?" Keel-Head chimes back. "Wait till them peanut shells come down on your head. Ha ha."

Tuf-Tuf laughs. "Hey, Vunga, you and me walking home together after?" he asks.

"Sure thing, man."

As the theatre fills up, the lady with the treats makes her first round in the balcony. Gabby and I both take a bag of asham. It is the best. As we wait for the movie to begin, I take in the surroundings. From the balcony, the roof of the theatre rises way above where we sit. The walls are covered with blue drapes all the way to the back of the pit. The walls in the pit area are painted black right up to the edge of the screen, which has purple curtains drawn across it . Anticipation builds in my heart as the lights in the theatre dim and the curtains draw open. As music begins to play, people in the pit erupt into shouting and dancing and clapping. I look at Keel-Head and ask, "What's that?"

"That's the best part," he says. "You wait and see."

I look at Gabby. I can tell he is confused too. We don't know what to expect. The theatre we go to with Aunt Beth is very quiet.

"Yes, man," Keel-Head assures me. "This is the best part of the show."

We keep watching. The screen comes alive with the trailers for upcoming movies. This quiets the crowd in the pit—that is, until the movie begins.

The Mark of Zorro flashes onto the screen. Loud cheers erupt when Zorro greets one of his servants while not wearing his disguise. Next, the masked Zorro gallops onto the screen riding his trusty horse, his sword held high, slashing a large Z into the sky. The pit breaks into sheer pandemonium:

"Faster, man!"

"Where you going?"

"Who you going to catch?"

"Watch out there, him on the rock back of you!"

"Turn round, turn round, quick, man!"

"Watch out, there's more in the tree!"

"You better listen now or you going to get killed!"

"Watch out behind you. Him going to jump on you!"

The house crowd is not far behind with shouts and encouragement and pure excitement. The chatter goes on during the whole show and then again during the Gene Autry western that starts as soon as *Zorro* ends. In the meantime, some of the house patrons chew pieces of paper into wads, which they launch with rubber bands into the pit section. This gets even more ruckus going as those the spit balls hit accuse other pit attendees and front row house patrons of doing it. This will make great fodder for the conversation on the way home.

Finally, the screen goes blank and the purple curtains close. It's time to go home. We all gather outside to look for friends so we can go home together. Those who travel by bus head eastward to the hill and then down the stone road on the other side to the Farmer's Market, where the buses wait for them. Others, like Keel-Head, walk in groups to their homes in the neighbourhoods around town, mostly on the hillsides. The rest of us—Mount-Up, Tuf-Tuf, Gabby, and I—gather together to start our journey to the countryside where there are no buses. Mount-Up lives on the side of the hill across from our family. We are a mixture of balcony, house and pit, but on the road home we are all united in one theme: rehashing the two movies until it's time to part. All is calm until we pass the high schools. The review begins when we are going up through Belmont, where the grade is steeper.

"Did you see Zorro get him, man?" Mount-Up asks in an excited voice.

Tuf-Tuf agrees. "Yeah man, he get him good. But say, you see how the bullet ping off the rock right by his head?"

"What you say, man?" Gabby chimes in. "Didn't you see it take some hair right off his head? That's what happened."

"You are right, you know," Mount-Up whispers.

Gabby's voice rises. "That Zorro, he is too good with his sword. He's just too good."

"What about Gene Autry?" I shout back. "He shot the button off the shirt of that rustler, didn't he?"

"Say what? When?" Gabby asks excitedly.

"Hey, Gabby, where you been?" Mount-Up chirps. "You are so blind. Ha, ha, ha. Ah got ya, hee hee."

"Man, it's music in your head," Tuf-Tuf shoots back. "Uh-huh. Say, man, it's the music messing you up."

This chatter goes on all the way up the hill where the roofs of houses are flush with the road. The hill rises almost straight up from the road. Trees and bushes cling to rocks and the odd house is carved into a crevice of the cliff. There, etched footpaths zigzag up to the small wooden structures that sit with one side on the ground and the other on stilts buried in the rock, daring the elements to challenge their existence.

We pass the road to Grand Anse Beach on the right, and shortly after, the mud road leading to the jail on the left. As we chatter, we scarcely notice we're walking down the other side of the hill to a flat area.

Suddenly, the air is still and all sounds vanish. We see the road to the sugarcane factory and slow down our pace. Quietly, we cross to the other side of the road, as far onto the grass as we can go without stepping into the ditch. We hold our breath, intent on passing the lonely house across the road from us without being noticed. Everyone knows the Shango Woman lives there.

I see a flash of light through the branches of the huge tree that stands like a sentinel protecting the Shango house.

My heart is pounding so madly I can hear it. *I wonder if the others can hear it too.* At that moment, a howling wind rushes through the large tree, sending its branches swaying wildly with lights flashing through them. Our feet freeze to the ground, our minds suspended mid-thought. I hear Gabby breathing loudly. Someone else is sniffling. My knees knock against each other. Tuf-Tuf whimpers like a puppy and Mount-Up mumbles a prayer.

"Run!" Gabby cries out.

We dash madly down the road with Tuf-Tuf leading the way and the rest of us in hot pursuit. After a while, we realize we're still together with no monster trying to catch us. We're on the other side of the Shango house, well on our way to the sugarcane factory.

Mount-Up, whose family just moved into the area, asks:

"What happen at that scary old house?"

Our parents have told Gabby and me to never speak of the Shango Woman, but Tuf-Tuf can't resist the opportunity to tell a tale.

"Me dad say the high priestess of the Shango cult had a son who take money from the house. When he come back, she ask him why he took the money. He lied, saying he not take her money."

He pauses for a breath. I can't resist either and take over the telling.

"The Shango woman put a curse on him, her own son, that his head will be buried in the sand. On Sunday morning some boys went to dive at the beach. When they climb up the diving board, they see a man with his head in the sand under the water."

"You don't say!" Mount-Up exclaims. "But the sand must be hard down under the sea, right?"

"That tells the power of the Shango people," Tuf-Tuf claims.

"That must be some powerful magic," I agree.

"Me for sure never passing there alone," Tuf-Tuf says.

"I still got to go up the hill to Morne Jaloux." Mount-Up's voice cracks. "And right now I feel real scared."

Dead silence. For sure we are all thinking the same thing: Mount-Up should not continue alone. But in the end, none of us offers to walk him up the hill.

VUNGA LEAVES HIS BELOVED ISLAND

14

GRENADA FAREWELL

93

The night before I left my beloved island, I felt very lonely. I tossed and turned for hours. Around midnight I got up and looked through the letters on the nightstand.

I remembered my father sitting at the head of the dining table as he usually did on Sundays.

"Walter, it's best for you to say your piece," Mother said.

We all waited for him to speak. My father cleared his throat. "Frank," he began.

My heart jumped. My father never called me anything but Vunga.

"Your mother and I have arranged for Herby to bring you to Canada."

I was shocked. "But why, Dad?"

I thought of the nice girl I had recently met on the bus and how I was thinking of inviting her to see the new Zorro movie.

"Son, it's best for you to get a good education like Herby."

My oldest brother had just completed his university studies and got a very good job right away.

"Don't worry," Mother said. "You will graduate from high school before you have to leave."

Unfortunately, my visa came early. It turned out I had to arrive in Canada sooner than my parents had expected. Three weeks later, I was on my way to Pearls Airport, my science and geometry exams unwritten.

When I boarded the plane, I stopped at the top of the stairs, looked back, and waved. Dad was weeping. That was the only time I had ever seen my father cry.

As soon as I got to Toronto, I wrote my parents a letter. In it I asked why Dad was crying. His reply was brief.

I know I'll never see you again.

And he never did. Two years later my father died of cancer of the spleen. His memory and the values he taught his children live with me still and come rushing back whenever I visit my beloved island.

FRANK'S ACKNOWLEDGEMENTS

I am truly grateful to Pearl, my soulmate and companion. My precious wife is the pillar of my life and the light that guides me through new adventures, all the while being my rudder, my booster, my editor, and my confidante. She found ways to pacify my galloping brain through storytelling and creativity.

A huge thank you to Lucio and Nadia, who despite living thousands of miles away gave me guidance in writing my personal stories. Closer to home, gratitude to our son Darren Banfield and his wonderful wife Michelle Willcott, whose feedback is deeply treasured. I am truly grateful to the London Writers Society and in particular to our critiquing group for sharing their vast knowledge and guiding me through my storytelling journey.

Also, my deepest gratitude to the caregivers of my youth: my sister Ermintrude Campbell, brother Herbert, and sisters Ada, Nellie St. Bernard, and Lyn-Eve Johnson.

Also heartfelt thanks to my other siblings: Rob, William, Daphne, Roy, Freddy, Joyce, Keith, and Adrian. Mom, Dad, and La-La, I now know you truly had your hands full raising me, yet you carried it off with panache. Your wise words have been with me throughout my adventures and mishaps. You are all forever in my heart.

And, of course, I will be forever grateful to Eva Parada for capturing the essence of Vunga and Gabby and the remarkable brotherhood they shared. I am grateful also to her parents and siblings, who supported her in this effort.

Thank you all for helping me on this journey.

EVA'S ACKNOWLEDGEMENTS

I cannot express how grateful I am to my parents, Damarys and Juan Carlos Parada. They have stood by my side throughout the making of this book. Also, they have been able to keep me in check even though my mind likes to wander away, and still love me unconditionally. I cannot thank them enough for their continuous support. I would not be able to do it without them.

Also, to Celeste (Abi) Parada. My sister and other half showed me what it means to be hardworking and strong. If it weren't for her constant cheering from here on earth and from above, I would not be where I am today.

The same love to my annoying yet amazing siblings, Tianna and Jared Parada, as well as to my sister-in-law and friend for life, Naomi Parada. Their loving encouragement has allowed me to finish this amazing project.

An enormous thanks to the writer, Frank Banfield, and his wonderful wife and editor, Pearl Lee. They have given me such an awesome and amazing opportunity. I have grown and learned so many things while working with them. They have shown me so much love and have been extremely patient, and they so kindly let me work flexibly since I was still in school.

Another big thanks to everyone that helped with the process, editing and guiding, as well as many other things for this book. Thank you for your hard work and wonderful talent to make these wondrous stories ready for the world.

HEARTFELT APPRECIATION TO:

Kayla Lang for her infinite patience and expertise as she guided us through the publishing process

Leanne whose editing skills clarified the text while preserving the authenticity of the dialect of Vunga's boyhood

Teresita for her clever and whimsical touches to the cover and interior

Jared Parada for his work on the franklypearlandeva.com book trailer

Darren, Michelle, Vitaliy, Maria, Nikita, and Valeria (Lera) for feedback on the cover

And a special shoutout to Alastair Henry who has cheered us on through the entire process

ABOUT FRANK AND EVA

Frank Banfield is a retired psychotherapist. A late bloomer, he graduated from McGill University with a Bachelor of Social Work degree in 1997 at age sixty-two. Then he and his wife taught English in China for three years. Back in Canada, Frank returned to McGill and graduated with his Master of Social Work degree. He and his wife are members of the London Writers Society and Canscaip Friends. *Vunga: Tales of an Island Boy* is his first book. The tales, illustrated by teen artist, Eva Parada, are suitable for older teens and adults, especially those who grew up as mischief makers.

Eva Parada spent much of her high school graduating year working on the Vunga illustrations. She has always been serious about drawing and is intrigued by how deeper emotions can be expressed without words. Eva is planning to study animation and art therapy. Her goal is to work with young children and their families, especially those who, like herself, have suffered similar experiences of illness and loss. When she's not drawing, Eva enjoys walking and listening to music.

You can contact Frank and Eva at:
franklypearlandeva.com

Printed in the USA
CPSIA information can be obtained
at www.ICGtesting.com
JSHW070743160424
61238JS00002B/2